Dana Clark

ANTON IN SHOW BUSINESS

a comedy by
Jane Martin

D1488797

SAMUEL FRENCH, INC.
45 WEST 25TH STREET   **NEW YORK 10010**
7623 SUNSET BOULEVARD   **HOLLYWOOD 90046**
LONDON   *TORONTO*

IMPORTANT BILLING AND CREDIT REQUIREMENTS

Anton in Show Business premiered at the Humana Festival of New American Plays in March 2000. It was directed by Jon Jory with the following cast:

T-Anne, Andwyneth, Don Blount ......Saidah Arrika Ekulona
Lisabette ....Monica Koskey
Casey ....Gretchen Lee Krich
Kate, Ben, Jackey ....Annette Helde
Ralph, Wikéwitch, Joe Bob ....Chick Reid
Holly ....Caitlin Miller
Joby ....Stacey Swift

Production Staff

Scenic Designer ....Paul Owen
Costume Designer ....Marcia Dixcy Jory
Lighting Designer ....Greg Sullivan
Sound Designer ....Martin R. Desjardins
Properties Designer ....Ben Hohman
Stage Manager ....Deb Acquavella
Production Assistant ....Amber Martin
Dramaturg ....Michael Bigelow Dixon
Assistant Dramaturg ....Ginna Hoben
Casting ....Laura Richin Casting

CAST

T-ANNE: The Stage Manager—also playing: Airport Announcer; Andwyneth; Don Blount; Gate Manager

ACTRESS #1: Kate; Ben; Jackey

ACTRESS #2: Ralph; Wikéwitch; Joe Bob

CASEY: 36 years old; tall, lean, plain

LISABETTE: 24 years old; charming and energetic

HOLLY: 30 years old. A drop-dead gorgeous TV star

JOBY: 26 years old. A recent graduate with an MFA in dramaturgy.

The play is performed by women in roles of both sexes.

SETTING

Various locations in New York and San Antonio
in the present.

There is one intermission.

DIRECTOR'S NOTE

It is possible to use a bare stage and minimal furniture. Many costumes must be rigged for quick change. You need six female scene changers/dressers, who handle the furniture moves and quick changes. Costume changes were full and were not done in sight. All changes were possible with the given text. I strongly suggest that you have the scene changers in several rehearsals prior to tech. Actors continued to play during scene changes. Have fun!

ACT I

(A bare stage. In the darkness, rolling thunder, and then suddenly cutting across it, lightning. The flashes illuminate a mysterious cloaked figure. Thunder. A special. The figure speaks.)

T. ANNE. The American theatre's in a shitload of trouble. *(Flash, crash.)* That's why the stage is bare, and it's a cast of six, one non-union. *(Flash, crash.)* I'm T-Anne, the stage manager, but I'm also in the play. *(Flash.)* Like a lot of plays you've seen at the end of the 20th century, we all have to play a lot of parts to make the whole thing economically viable... *(Crash.)...* HOMAGE TO THORNTON WILDER. *(Flash, crash. She drops the cloak. She wears blue jeans, a T-shirt, many keys at her belt.)* The date is *(date)*, 2000, just before noon. Well, I'll show you a little bit about how our profession is laid out. Up around here are the Broadway theatres, sort of between 42nd and 52nd Street, we like to think that's the heart of everything. City of New York, State of New York, United States of America, the world, the galaxy, the universe. Down over here is Greenwich Village, around there we do off-Broadway, that's good too. Now Tribeca, Soho, Lower East Side, we call that the "downtown scene," off-off stuff. An incredibly colorful group of people who despise realism and have all won the Obie Award... that's good too. Beyond that, radiating out in all directions for thousands of miles is something called "regional theatre," which I understand once showed a lot of promise but has since degenerated into dying medieval fiefdoms and arrogant baronies producing small-cast comedies, cabaret musicals, mean-spirited new plays and the occasional deconstructed classic, which everybody hates. After that, moving west, we reach the burning, uninhabitable desert and its militias who don't go to plays, and beyond that, singing a siren call, the twin evil kingdoms of Flic and Tube, the bourne from which no traveler returns. Now back to New York, thank God. Let's see, the Empire State Building, the Statue of Liberty and the Actors' Equity offices... that's our union. They make sure no more than 80% of our membership is out of work on any given day. And over there... yes, right over there is where we worship, yes sir, *The New York Times.* Well, that's about it. Now, with a short subway ride we get to one of the audition studios where producers and theatres come to find actors for their plays. Here's the front door, elevator up to the fifth floor, Studio C, where the San Antonio, Texas Actors Express has come to the big city to cast *The Three Sisters* by Anton Chekhov. He's Russian. At noon, you can always hear the actors doing their vocal warm-ups. *(Vocal warm-ups can be heard.)* Aya—there they are. Not much happens before noon. Theatre folks sleep late. So, another day's begun. There's Lisabette Cartwright walking into Studio C. She graduated from SMU (Southern Methodist) drama department and began teaching third grade. Then she was invited to New York for an audition because the producer once had her appendix removed by one of her uncles. Lisabette's really excited, and her mom, who is at this moment canning okra, is too. Over there is Casey Mulgraw, the one dressed in the skirt/pants, skirt/pants thing, a lot of people call her the Queen of off-off Broadway. She's a little hung over because she just celebrated the opening of her 200th play without ever having been paid a salary. She also has a yeast infection that is really pissing her off. In our town, we like to know the facts about everybody.

(NOTE: All scene and costume changes are done by six female "changers," dressed in a variety of contemporary styles, but all in black. T-Anne, the stage manager, moves to a small out-of-the-way table where she sits and follows the script. Three folding chairs are placed to create the waiting room of Studio C. CASEY, a woman of 36, waits. LISABETTE, 24, enters. She has a rolling suitcase.)

LISABETTE. Hi. *(CASEY nods.)* Is this the Studio C waiting room for Actors Express? *(CASEY nods.)* *Three Sisters* audition? *(CASEY nods.)* Oh, my heavens, it's so humid! I feel like I'm oiled up for the beach or something. I surely admire your fortitude in wearing both skirt and pants. Bet you're auditioning for Olga, huh?

CASEY. Why? Because Olga is older and homely and a spinster and has no life of her own and thus has assumed the role of caregiver to her brother and it's usually thought to be the least interesting acting role of *The Three Sisters.* Would that be it?

LISABETTE. Well, no, I...

CASEY. It's what you meant.

LISABETTE. I think I'll just start over. *(She does.)* Hi.

CASEY. Hi.

LISABETTE. I'm Lisabette Cartwright, from La Vernia, Texas. Graduated SMU but then I taught third grade for two years, bein' scared of an actor's life, and Maple Elementary loved me and wants me back anytime, but in a dream the Lord himself reaffirmed my calling so I made my comeback in *Fiddler on the Roof* but this is my first New York audition and I'm so jumpy my breasts bob even when I walk real slow. What's your name?

CASEY. Casey Mulgraw, one of my breasts had to be surgically removed because of a malignancy and I seem to be in remission but who knows how long that will last.

LISABETTE. Oh, my G-o-o-d-d-d!

CASEY. Want to do one more take?

LISABETTE. No, I would like you to forgive me for bein' such a dipshit, pardon the language, Jesus. I'm real sorry for your troubles and it looks to me like they did a real good match.

CASEY. *(Chuckles.)* And yes, I'm reading for Olga for the obvious reasons.

LISABETTE. Really, I think Olga is the most spiritual of all the sisters.

CASEY. Good try. You don't have a smoke by any chance?

LISABETTE. Ummmm, I don't.

CASEY. Cough drop?

LISABETTE. Beef jerky.

CASEY. No thanks.

LISABETTE. I'm auditioning for Masha.

CASEY. The dark, passionate, amoral poetess. I feel dark; men call me passionate; I'm definitely amoral, and I've actually had several poems published but they never, never, never let me read for that part.

LISABETTE. Because you're a little plain?

CASEY. Thank you for speaking the unspeakable.

LISABETTE. I did it again, huh? I'm, oh my, very nervous but that's just no excuse. I would like to say I'm in way over my head and could I have a hug?

CASEY. *(Not unkindly.)* If it's absolutely necessary.

(They hug. The stage manager enters to speak to the actors. A rolling door might divide the spaces. Behind her, a table with three chairs is set up as the audition room. RALPH BRIGHTLY, an English director, and KATE, the producer, are at the table. In a third chair, to the side, sits HOLLY SEABÉ, a TV goddess who is pre-cast as IRINA and is helping audition.)

STAGE MANAGER. Ms. Todoravskia is ready to see you both.

CASEY. Both?

STAGE MANAGER. Both. Hustle it up, we're running behind.

LISABETTE. *(Still in the anteroom. To CASEY.)* Do they usually see actors in groups?

CASEY. No. And we're not a group.

(CASEY and LISABETTE enter the audition room.)

KATE. *(Rising.)* Hi. I am Katrina Todoravskia, Producing Director of Actors Express. And you are?

LISABETTE. Me?

KATE. You.

LISABETTE. I'm sorry, I forgot the question.

CASEY. Your name.

LISABETTE. Oh, Lisabette Cartwright.

(KATE kisses LISABETTE's hand extended for a shake.)

KATE. You are devastatingly beautiful. *(Turns to CASEY.)* And I gather you're here to audition for Olga?

CASEY. How'd you guess?

KATE. You look like an Olga.

CASEY. Thanks.

KATE. This is the play's director, Ralph Brightly; he runs the Toads Hall Rep in London.

RALPH. *(Shaking hands.)* Well, a stone's throw outside, really. *(Shakes LISABETTE's hand.)* Charmed. *(Shakes CASEY's hand.)* Pleased.

KATE. *(Gesturing toward HOLLY.)* And this is...

LISABETTE. Oh my G-o-o-d-d, you're Holly Seabé. I can't believe it! Holly Seabé. I love your TV show! Your character is so kooky and glamorous. You have such great timing. I've learned practically everything I know about foreplay from that show. You are so liberated!

HOLLY. Thanks.

LISABETTE. Oh my God, pardon me Jesus, are you going to be *in* the play?

HOLLY. Irina.

LISABETTE. *(Clapping her hands.)* She's going to be in the play. This is way cool! *(To CASEY.)* Isn't that cool?

CASEY. *(Smiling, but a bit reserved.)* Yes, cool.

HOLLY. Thanks.

LISABETTE. I am so stoked!

RALPH. Yes, well, off we go then. *Three Sisters*, as you know, by Anton Pavlovitch himself. I'll just drop some breadcrumbs along the path before we hear you...

KATE. Running 40 minutes behind.

RALPH. Right. Straight along. Give you the gist in five words. Funny, funny, funny, funny, tragic.

CASEY. We're referring to *Three Sisters*?

RALPH. *The Three Sisters,* yes.

CASEY. Funny, funny, funny, tragic?

RALPH. *Funny*, funny, funny, *funny,* tragic.

CASEY. Okay, I can do that.

LISABETTE. Do what?

CASEY. Show him that in our auditions.

LISABETTE. Gee, I didn't think it was funny.

RALPH. Precisely, that's to be our little revelation.

KATE. Forty minutes late.

RALPH, Right then, on we go.

(A young woman in the audience rises and says:)

JOBY. Excuse me.

RALPH. Let's get cracking.

JOBY. Excuse me.

(The actors glance up, confused. The "director" tries to go on.)

RALPH, It's Chekhov, don't you see, so we're certainly not ready to do text...

JOBY. *(From the audience.)* Excuse me.

(The actors stop. They look to KATE.)

KATE. Yes?

JOBY. Is the director... ummm ...

RALPH. *(Supplying the character name.)* Ralph.

JOBY. Right, Ralph. Is it supposed to be a man played by a woman?

KATE. Yes. *(To RALPH.)* Go on.

JOBY. How come?

RALPH. You mean why am I playing a man?

JOBY. I mean what's the point?

RALPH. Could you possibly sit down and let us act?

KATE. Wait. *(To JOBY.)* Hi.

JOBY. Hi.

KATE. What's your name?

JOBY. Joby. But I...

KATE. Joby, we want to thank you for coming to the theatre; we need young audiences.

RALPH. But...

KATE. Shhhh. Now you'll understand this as a woman, Joby...

RALPH. Could she please...

(KATE silences RALPH with a look.)

KATE. Eighty percent of the roles in the American theatre are played by men, and 90% of the directors *are* men. The point of having a male director played by a woman is to redress the former and satirize the latter. How's that?

JOBY. *(After a brief pause.)* Okay.

(JOBY sits down. KATE nods at RALPH.)

RALPH. Right. Onward and upward, eh? *(He looks at CASEY.)* What I'd like you to do, sweetie, is use only the word "tiddlypee" as text... *(He looks at LISABETTE.)* And you, dear, will say only "tiddlypoo." With these words, we will now play the scene where Masha tells Olga she's leaving her husband Kulygin and leaving town with the soldier Vershinin.

CASEY. But there is no such scene.

RALPH. Yes, precisely.

CASEY. So why?

RALPH. *(Sweetly.)* You don't wish to audition?

CASEY. That's the answer to "why?"

RALPH. Look, dear...

(LISABETTE, trying to circumvent the oncoming conflict, goes into the improvisation.)

LISABETTE. *(You wished to see me?)* Tiddlypoo, tiddlypoo?

CASEY. *(Is it true you and Vershinin are in love?)* Tiddlypee, tiddlypee, tiddlypee... tiddlypee?

LISABETTE. *(I am leaving Kulygin and going away with Vershinin.)* Tiddlypoo, tiddlypoo... tiddlypoo... tiddlypoo, tiddlypoo, tiddlypoo, tiddlypoo.

CASEY. *(If you go, what will happen to me?)* Tiddlypee... tiddlypee, tiddlypee, tiddlypee?

LISABETTE. *(You'll be fine.)* Tiddlypoo, tiddlypoo.

CASEY. *(To RALPH.)* How am I supposed to know what she's saying?

RALPH. Well, that would be the heart of the audition, wouldn't it?

(CASEY tries once more.)

CASEY. *(If you go, we'll be left with Natasha!)* Tiddlypee, tiddlypee... tiddlypee, tiddlypee. *(She stops.)* Look, this is ridiculous.

RALPH. *(Coolly.)* Really?

CASEY. Well, yes, really. Can't we just do a scene using the script? I mean that would be sensible, right?

RALPH. Perhaps to an American actress, dear.

CASEY. *(Not happy.)* Ummmmmm...

LISABETTE. Oh, but this is fun. Don't you think it's fun? It's kind of interesting.

CASEY. *(Slow burn.)* American actress.

LISABETTE. *(Feeling the tension.)* Just really, really, really, really fun!

CASEY. *(Burning.)* You know, Ralph ... dear... you Brits are arrogant, pompous, chauvinistic, smug, insufferable boors who take jobs from American actors and directors because of the toadying of the American press and the Anglophile American rich, and I've seen Chekhov done in London that really smelled up the place with its stiff-upper-lip, over practical, no-self-pity-or-despair-here-darling style that has nothing, nothing to do with Russian passion or spiritual darkness, so...

JOBY. Excuse me.

CASEY. *(Still on the emotional high.)* What?! What do you want?

KATE. Easy

JOBY. Isn't this all just a little self-referential?

KATE. I'm sorry, Joby, but we are trying to perform a play and...

JOBY. I mean it's all just about the theatre. Isn't that a little precious?

KATE. Why?

JOBY. Well, theatre people talking about theatre.

KATE. As opposed to theatre people talking about the international monetary fund or the cloning of sheep?

JOBY. Well, is theatre culturally important enough to be the subject of a play?

RALPH. Nice of you to buy a ticket.

JOBY. Actually, they're comps.

RALPH. Ah.

JOBY. I'd think your only hope is to work on a deeply personal and profoundly emotional level.

CASEY. Well, the thing about the Brits is very emotional.

RALPH. And plays aren't ordinarily deeply personal until after the exposition.

JOBY. Oh.

CASEY. Later on, the play takes hold, and there is devastating loss and a lot of really profound metaphors that will knock your socks off. I mean, *knock your socks off!*

JOBY. Oh.

CASEY. Okay?

JOBY. *(A brief pause.)* Fine.

(She sits down.)

CASEY. *(Going back.)* ... with its stiff-upper-lip, over-practical, no-self-pity-or-despair-here-darling style that has nothing, nothing to do with Russian passion or spiritual darkness. So don't give me that American actress crap!

(A tense moment.)

RALPH. Right. Nicely done. I think I've seen more than enough. Thanks ever so for coming in.

LISABETTE. We're finished?

RALPH. Lovely work, sweetie. *(Turning to CASEY, smiling.)* And I quite agree with you, dear, when Americans do Chekhov, it's just awash in self-pity.

(CASEY gives him the finger and stalks out.)

LISABETTE. Well, anyway, this was my first professional audition, and it was really a lot of fun, and I want to thank you for calling me in and I really hope to work for you someday and... *(She begins to cry.)* ... and I'm sorry I'm crying. I didn't mean to cry, and I've never even been to London but... she's right, you're a real jerk.

(LISABETTE runs out, leaving RALPH, KATE and HOLLY alone.)

RALPH. *(Ironically.)* Well, that was a breath of fresh air.

KATE. Ralph, I want to apologize to you as an American...

RALPH, No, no...

KATE. I've seen hundreds, thousands of auditions, and I never...

RALPH. No need, sweetie...

KATE. I mean, who do they think they are?

RALPH. Made their beds, haven't they? Fat chance they'll be getting any work from this old British fairy.

(KATE laughs appreciatively.)

HOLLY. I liked them. *(They turn to look at her.)* I've been treated like dirt in situations like this, but now I'm rich and famous and you need me so you're sort of shit out of luck, huh?

So here's the deal: I liked them and I'm bored with auditions so they're over and those two are in our play.

RALPH. Miss Seabé, they do not have the requisite talent.

HOLLY. Well, neither do I so maybe nobody will notice. *(She starts to exit.)* One thing, though. The little sweet one from Texas should play Irina, and I'll play Masha. Oh, and the Olga... well, she's Olga. Tiddlypee, tiddlypoo.

RALPH. So, Kate, love, I gather that's the horse that pulls our custard wagon, eh?

KATE. Well...

RALPH. Not to worry. In the kingdom of the barbarians, shit tastes like veal.

(Lights change. Furniture is removed as CASEY and LISABETTE move into two specials, where they talk to their mothers on the "phone.")

LISABETTE. Ma? It's me, Lisabette...

CASEY. Mother, okay, don't go ballistic...

LISABETTE. I got it! I got it! I got it! I got the part!

CASEY. Yes, I know I'm thirty-six years old, and I still have $40,000 in student loans...

LISABETTE. Ma, Ma, wait, no there's more...

CASEY. Yes, I would have to leave my day job...

LISABETTE. I'm gonna act with a TV star!

CASEY. Okay, the real deal...

LISABETTE. Holly Seabé! Yes! Me and Holly Seabé; can you believe it?

CASEY. Yes, it's kind of a crappy part; it's some hick town in Texas; the salary is like pesos; I'll lose my job; you won't have anybody to abuse but, lest we forget here, I'm supposed to be an actress!

LISABETTE. Ma, it's Chekhov!

CASEY. Mother...

LISABETTE. He's a Russian.

CASEY. Mother...

LISABETTE. No, it's beautiful and wise and sad, and I get to be a real professional!

CASEY. Screw you! Mother!

LISABETTE. Love you, Ma!

CASEY. *(Hanging up.)* Damnit!

LISABETTE. *(Hanging up.)* Yes!

(Two connected plane seats are brought on. LISABETTE and CASEY move to sit in them. We hear an airport announcement.)

GATE ANNOUNCER. Flight number 270 to San Antonio, Texas, gate 27B, boarding is now complete. Flight number 270. All passengers...

CASEY. My dad's great. I worked weekends for a thousand years in his hardware store.

LISABETTE. You are kidding!

CASEY. What kidding?

LISABETTE. My dad has a hardware store.

CASEY. Yeah?

LISABETTE. You sorted screws?

CASEY. Oh yeah. *(They smile.)* Your dad want you to run it?

LISABETTE. Me? No. He sold it. He works in a community center.

CASEY. Well, my dad wants me. I dream I take it over and I wake up, stapled to 3/4 inch plywood, screaming. Okay, the hardware connection.

LISABETTE. You're not married, right?

CASEY. I'm not married, right. You?

LISABETTE. I can't abide sex.

CASEY. Oh.

LISABETTE. Well, temporarily. I've kinda had some bad luck.

CASEY. Doesn't hold me back.

LISABETTE. I was kinda doin' it with my high school boyfriend in the back of his car, an' we were hit from behind by a drunk in a pickup.

CASEY. Ouch.

LISABETTE. They said they'd never seen that kind of whiplash.

CASEY. Sorry.

LISABETTE. Meanwhile, back at school I was kind of bein' forced into an affair by my history teacher an' just after that I was sort of halfway raped by a plumber.

CASEY. *(Horrified.)* Jesus.

LISABETTE. No, it wasn't too bad really. I had to deal, y'know? The only bad part was for three years I couldn't touch a man, even like a handshake, without throwing up. Projectile vomiting, so there were some awkward moments at parties.

CASEY. You're kidding me, right?

LISABETTE. No, really, it wasn't so bad. I'm over it, except really, really occasionally when I first meet people. How about your relationships?

CASEY. A lot of casual sex.

LISABETTE. Really.

CASEY. A lot. Always with members of the cast. And I've done 200 plays off-off.

LISABETTE. Wow.

CASEY. Outside of rehearsal, I'm actually a virgin.

LISABETTE. Wow.

CASEY. Of course, I'm always in rehearsal.

LISABETTE. Oh, I really respect that. I'm a virgin too. Except for being harassed, whiplashed, and on New Year's Eve.

(HOLLY enters from first class.)

CASEY. Hi.

LISABETTE. Oh my God.

HOLLY. I saw you guys when you came through first class.

LISABETTE. We walked right by you!?

HOLLY. No problem. I was enjoying some brain surgeon hitting on me.

LISABETTE. Excuse me, but... shoot ... I just want to say that when Kate, the producer person, made me the offer... well... she said you had put in a word for us... me and Casey... Casey and I... God, I am such a hick, Pardon me Jesus, anyway... thank you, thank you, thank you!

CASEY. It was really nice.

HOLLY. Well, hey, yeah I did, thanks but, you know, I was like nobody once too. Really down on the food chain like you guys... ummm... I won't even tell you the stuff I went through. Well, okay, the easy stuff was being told I had no talent like that director piranha said about you, right? And my deal was that talent isn't the point here... I mean, we're going to whatever Texas or wherever. Like, nobody who is anybody will see us or care. Maybe excepting my manager who has time for one client, me, and who would not care diddly dick if you guys had talent or not. *(A brief awkwardness.)* But the point is you didn't think *I* meant you had no talent, did you?

CASEY. No, no.

LISABETTE. No, no.

HOLLY. Because you can understand I have no way of knowing that. I mean ... tiddlypee, tiddlypoo.

LISABETTE. Right.

CASEY. Right.

HOLLY. My point is you guys were disrespected and he had to pay.

CASEY. You mean...

HOLLY. I mean, once they said you had no talent, I had to see you were hired.

LISABETTE. Wow.

HOLLY. Because I had that pulled on me, and now that *will not happen* in my presence. Like I'm the respect police.

CASEY. Thanks.

HOLLY. No problem. So I just wanted to shed a little light.

LISABETTE. That is really so nice.

CASEY. Just think, all of us have been told we have no talent.

HOLLY. Exactly!

CASEY. Well, that's something to build on.

HOLLY. Yeah, that's the other thing. We have to stick together down there in...

CASEY. Texas.

LISABETTE. Oh absolutely.

HOLLY. Because I have this intuition it's going to be like combat, but we stick together, we make them pay.

LISABETTE. Like we were three sisters.

HOLLY. That is so sweet and so right. That like zaps my guts.

CASEY. There's an empty seat.

HOLLY. Nah, I got to go back, I don't eat pretzels.

LISABETTE. We're talking about guys.

HOLLY. Them I eat. See you later.

(HOLLY leaves. Three folding chairs are set, facing two other chairs for the next scene. Please remember the changes are cinematic. We never stop or take the lights out for a change.)

T-ANNE. Please place your seats and tray tables in an upright position; we are beginning our descent into San Antonio.

*(We are now in the rehearsal room on the first day. KATE,
CASEY, HOLLY, LISABETTE and the new director, an
African American woman named ANDWYNETH
WYORÉ.)*

KATE. *(Addressing them.)* Actors Express. Get it? Express?
We are a serious theatre. We are unique. What is our artistic
policy? Well, I can state that policy clearly. We live these ideas.
At Actors Express, we call them the Seven Virtues. Number
one, we do plays that... *(She makes a complex gesture.)* Two:
our style is surgically defined as... *(A series of sounds.)* And
only that. Fourthly, multi-cultural new works from the classical
repertoire that say to the audience... *(An even more complex
gesture.)* So that, in summation, or, seventh, we can say... *(She
stares at the ceiling, thinking.)* and we say that with no fear of
being misunderstood. Oh, I know, this policy makes us contro-
versial. We offend, we pique, we challenge while at the same
time bringing together, healing, and making our community one.
In a nutshell. This unique mission has made us essential to San
Antonio, not because... is there something out the window?
CASEY. Sorry.
KATE. Not because I have the best education money can
buy...
LISABETTE. Wow.
KATE. Stanford, Harvard, Yale, but because... *(HOLLY is
doctoring her lipstick.)* Holly, if you give this a chance, I think
you'll find it's crucial to our work.
HOLLY. Stanford, Harvard, Yale...
KATE. Precisely.
HOLLY. *(Pointing at herself.)* Biddyup High, Biddyup,
Nebraska.
KATE. But because... hear this... contemporary relevance.
CASEY. Contemporary relevance.
KATE. Contemporary relevance.

CASEY. Yes.

KATE. Our raison d'être! Does anyone find what I said moving? *(LISABETTE raises her hand.)* Because I am moved, and it is central to our aesthetic. *(LISABETTE applauds.)* Now I wanted to meet with you, our three sisters, before the rest of our cast arrived, to bond as sisters and to achieve a... It's now my pleasure to introduce our director, Andwyneth Wyoré, Artistic Director of San Antonio's Black Rage.

HOLLY. Doesn't that happen between countries?

KATE. Excuse me?

HOLLY. Cultural exchange?

ANDWYNETH. *(Chuckling.)* You got that right, girl.

KATE. Interestingly enough, Andwyneth also went to Stanford, Harvard, and Yale.

ANDWYNETH. 'Course I went free.

CASEY. What happened to the Brit?

KATE. Well, there were...

KATE/ANDWYNETH/HOLLY. Artistic differences.

ANDWYNETH. Uh-huh.

KATE. And I came to feel a sister...

ANDWYNETH. Girl, I'm not your sister. My momma see you, she faint, girl. She smack my daddy with an iron skillet! Huh-uh, baby, we got a little mutual use goin'. How about that? Down here in San Antonio you get some black people, some white people in the same room, there's always some foundation goes orgasmic. *(Cries deep in the act of sex.)* Multicultural! Multicultural! Yes! Yes!! Multicultural!! *(Back to her own voice.)* Pay a little rent, right? Suck a little green. Hey, I never did no white play, dig? Y'all a mystery to me, but I tell you one thing on Brother Chekhov, he just talk, talk, talk, talk, talk! Lord have mercy!

KATE, Well yes, but...

ANDWYNETH. Whine, whine, whine. Man, he got the self-pity diarrhea! Gushin' it out all over! Cut all that shit, X it out! Get down on the race question, down on the poverty question, get down on abuse of power, baby! No more, "Whine and dine with Brother Chekhov." Huh-uh. We gonna heat this sucker up! No script, huh-uh. I don't do script. Hell with that! What I see is a little white sisters thing, an' a black peasants thing. Little dance drama thing, little street corner doo-wap. *(HOLLY raises hand.)* S'up, girl?

HOLLY. I'm doing the script.

ANDWYNETH. You didn't follow the conversation?

HOLLY. Yeah, I can follow it, but I'm not doing that.

ANDWYNETH. Who the hell are you, girl?

HOLLY. You watch TV?

ANDWYNETH. Hell no, colored people all live in a cave.

HOLLY. I'm a big TV star.

ANDWYNETH. Well girl, you just pat yourself right on the back.

HOLLY. They begged me to come down here to wherever Texas to do a classic-style play. I don't give a shit about the race question or the poverty question. I don't have those problems. I got the film problem. I need to do film. No film, no respect. It's kind of like the race problem only in show business.

ANDWYNETH. You crazy, huh?

HOLLY. Yeah. So the rap is, you do TV you can't act. So my manager says to go backdoor. Get a little respect. Chekhov, Shakespeare, that stuff gives you shine. So like then you're a classical actress with fabulous breasts, and you can segue into sci-fi, action, cop-schlock, meet-cute or any genre.

ANDWYNETH. Let's cut to the bottom line, sister.

HOLLY. I'm saying every syllable Chekhov wrote, slow and clear.

ANDWYNETH. See, you are so far from my trip I can't even find you on the map.

HOLLY. Ms. Wyoré, the real difference between the two of us isn't what you think.

ANDWYNETH. Well, little thing, you bring it on.

HOLLY. The real difference is, you're fired.

(ANDWYNETH looks at KATE.)

KATE. *(At a loss.)* Well...

HOLLY. Trust me.

ANDWYNETH. You are one straight-up, no kiddin' around, in-your-face, don't misunderstand-me, bitch.

HOLLY. Sometimes, things just don't ... work out.

ANDWYNETH. *(Focusing on KATE.)* What are you, in-visible?

KATE. Ummmmm...

ANDWYNETH. She's the deal, or you're the deal?

(HOLLY also focuses on KATE.)

KATE. *(Finally, to ANDWYNETH.)* She's the deal.

ANDWYNETH. You get me down here, whip up a little money on my color, cast a buncha white girls an' then blow me off 'cause this prime-time toots shows up? *(To KATE.)* I'm gonna pin "racist" to your ass, Momma. They gonna burn you in the public square to get right with my people. There won't be nothin' left of you but little snowy white ashes, dig? You an' Chekhov is both toast!

(ANDWYNETH exits.)

KATE. Ummm... if you'll excuse me.

(KATE exits to talk to ANDWYNETH. The sisters are silent for a moment.)

CASEY. Anyone want some Skittles?

LISABETTE. You just fired the director in front of the producer without asking.

HOLLY. I am saying the lines.

CASEY. She's saying the lines.

HOLLY. Directors are a very gray area for me. It has been my experience that they actually like to be fired because they suffer from severe performance anxiety. They have these pushy little egos but hardly any usable information, which makes them very sad and time-consuming. I wouldn't worry because after you fire them, they usually find successful careers on cruise ships where they are completely harmless.

LISABETTE. But to do that, is that ethical?

HOLLY. Lisabette, I like you. I do. You seem like a very nice person. I'm not a very nice person, but I can still appreciate one when I see her.

LISABETTE. Thanks.

HOLLY. In college plays, community stuff, arty nowheresville professional gigs like this, there is probably something called ethics, but up where the eagles fly and the wolves run, up where American presidents screw the actresses, there is only power. The ethics thing is a little foggy. Power, on the other hand, is clear, it's clear, it's understood. For a very short time, Lisabette, here in wherever-it-is Texas, you will fly with an eagle. Say whoosh.

LISABETTE. Whoosh.

HOLLY. Enjoy.

(At this moment, BEN SHIPWRIGHT, a craggy actor enters. He is playing Vershinin.)

BEN. Hello, ladies.

LISABETTE. Hi.

CASEY. Hi.

HOLLY. Hi.

BEN. Ben Shipwright. Gonna play Vershinin.

CASEY. Olga, the boring sister.

LISABETTE. Masha. But I can't shake your hand right now. I'll explain later.

HOLLY. Masha.

LISABETTE. You're playing Masha?

HOLLY. We'll talk. Where are you from, Ben?

BEN. Right around here. I do some acting but I actually make my living singing country.

LISABETTE. Oh my God, you're Ben Shipwright?

BEN. Yeah.

LISABETTE. Oh my God, I love your records!

HOLLY. You record?

BEN. Little bit.

LISABETTE. Little bit? This week he has two singles in Top 50 Country!

HOLLY. Really?

CASEY. Mazeltov.

BEN. *(To HOLLY and CASEY.)* You girls from New York?

CASEY. Yeah.

HOLLY. L.A.

BEN. *(To LISABETTE.)* Now I know *you're* a home girl.

LISABETTE. *How* do you know?

BEN. Well, you talk San Antonio and you listen to a bunch of no-good pickers like me.

HOLLY. Ben?

BEN. Yes ma'am.

HOLLY. This relationship thing that goes down between Masha and Vershinin? We probably should get together and talk that out.

BEN. Be my pleasure. I'll let y'all get settled.

(BEN starts to exit.)

HOLLY. Dinner?

BEN. I'm sorry, you speakin' to me?

HOLLY. I was speaking to you.

BEN. Well... ummm... I don't believe I caught your name.

HOLLY. Holly Seabé.

BEN. Well, Miss Seabé, I got me a couple of kids want me to barbecue some ribs tonight.

(Starts to exit.)

HOLLY. Drink later?

BEN. Well, ummm, no ma'am. No ma'am, I can't. No offense intended.

HOLLY. *(Smiling, but not pleased.)* Really?

BEN. No ma'am, I better not. My wife...

HOLLY. How old are your kids?

BEN. Four and seven. Seven and a half.

HOLLY. Won't they be asleep?

BEN. *(They regard each other.)* Just no-can-do, ma'am. *(Shakes her hand.)* Real pleased to meet you. Lookin' forward to rehearsal. Catch y'all later.

(BEN exits.)

LISABETTE. I don't think he knew who you were! Can you believe that? I mean, you are on the cover of TV Guide!

HOLLY. I'll have to buy him a copy.

LISABETTE. But, am I right or am I wrong, he is really cute!

CASEY. My take is if you... *(She indicates HOLLY.)* ... come on to a guy, looking the way you do, and he stiffs you while talking about his kids, he is *really* unavailable.

HOLLY. If I come on to a guy... and I'm not saying I did... that guy can kiss his previous life goodbye for as long as I find said guy entertaining. And on this I would be willing to wager some fairly serious money.

CASEY. I think serious money to me and serious money to you could be seriously different.

LISABETTE. But what about his wife and kids?

HOLLY and CASEY. Shhh.

HOLLY. Okay, forget the money thing. We'll bet hair. Loser shaves her head.

LISABETTE. Wow.

CASEY. You can't afford to shave your head.

HOLLY. I won't have to.

CASEY. The guy's straight from Norman Rockwell.

HOLLY. I could screw anybody Norman Rockwell ever drew.

LISABETTE. This is so yeasty!

CASEY. Let's get it on.

(CASEY holds out her hand. HOLLY shakes it.)

HOLLY. He's going down.

LISABETTE. You aren't Baptist, huh?

HOLLY. Hey, Lisabette?

LISABETTE. Uh-huh?

HOLLY. I'm going to play Masha because it's the best part, and the most powerful person plays the best part. That's one of Hollywood's ten commandments. You'll play Irina, because I say so, but also because she's the youngest and you're the youngest and you would be really good doing her because you have yet to become a completely calcified diva.

LISABETTE. *(Not at all upset.)* Okay.

HOLLY. Everything's copasetic. Hey, let's go to the apartment hotel and get settled in fleabag hell and then find some cowboy dive with pine paneling and get unbelievably plotzed before tomorrow's first rehearsal, because I need to be hung over to face whatever director she digs up next.

(A scene change starts. Eventually, there will be two single beds, two chairs and a rolling door in place. This scene is played during the change.)

JOBY. *(From the audience.)* Excuse me. *(Scene change continues.)* Excuse me.

T-ANNE. What?

JOBY. Well, I... didn't you...

T-ANNE. Hey, spit it out; I'm busy.

JOBY. Well, didn't you consider that role offensive?

T-ANNE. Did you notice we're doing a scene change?

JOBY. Golly, as a person of color...

T-ANNE. You're a person of color?

JOBY. No, you are.

T-ANNE. Ooooo, I hate it when I forget.

JOBY. But, wasn't that... *(Whispers.)* ... stereotyped behavior?

T-ANNE. *(Again stopping her work.)* Listen, I have to... all right, okay... listen, Babyface, I would like to do something, almost anything, where nice white people like you didn't feel like they had to defend me. Particularly... *(Whispers back.)* .... in the middle of a scene change.

(T-ANNE goes back to work.)

JOBY. But it satirizes your political...

T-ANNE. Got to go.

JOBY. But, aren't you...

T-ANNE. No, I'm not. Want to know why?

JOBY. Oh, I do.

T-ANNE. 'Cause if I didn't do the plays that offended my color or politics or sex or religion or taste, I'd be shit out of work. Lights!

(T-ANNE exits. The scene light snaps on. JOBY is still standing.)

CASEY. *(To JOBY, not unkindly.)* Sit down, Joby. *(Starting the scene.)* I am *leveled* by the last drink. I am, as my beloved father would say, schnockered. *(Sings.)* Tell me I can't sing Karaoke?

HOLLY. You can't sing Karaoke.

LISABETTE. This is so amazing, it's like a pajama party.

HOLLY. *(Patting her knee.)* It is a pajama party.

LISABETTE. I mean, here I am, just out of drama school, and I am completely drunk, talking with real actors in a real way, including a great actress of the stage and a great actress from TV, and it just makes me want to cry.

HOLLY. Don't cry. Where did the vodka go?

LISABETTE. Holly, can I ask you a question?

HOLLY. Here it is.

(HOLLY pours herself another drink.)

LISABETTE. It's something about acting.

HOLLY. I don't know anything about acting.

LISABETTE. Okay then, have you had breast implants?

HOLLY. Yes.

LISABETTE. Yes?!

HOLLY. Yes.

CASEY. That actually makes me feel better.

HOLLY. I have had seventeen separate surgical procedures

to make me the completely natural beauty you see before
you. They have even reshaped my toes because I do a lot of
swimsuit.

LISABETTE. Those are artificial toes?

HOLLY. They are not artificial, they have been slimmed.

CASEY. How much?

HOLLY. Altogether?

CASEY. For the toes?

HOLLY. Seventeen thousand dollars.

LISABETTE. Wow.

CASEY. How much would it take to make me beautiful?

HOLLY. You're serious?

CASEY. Yeah.

HOLLY. Take off the sweatshirt.

(CASEY does.)

LISABETTE. But beauty is subjective.

HOLLY. Not in Hollywood. Stand up and turn around. Over
here. Over here, over here. *(CASEY does.)* Look at the ceiling.
(She does.) Hold your arms out like wings. Look left. Look
right. Okay. I could be off 10, even 15% here depending on
bone and muscle structure, but my estimate would be $600,000.

CASEY. Go ahead, flatter me.

HOLLY. Oh, there are divas who have paid more, and the
kicker is even then there's no guarantee the camera loves you.

LISABETTE. Oh my God.

HOLLY and CASEY. Pardon me Jesus.

CASEY. I'm giving it one more year.

(CASEY refreshes her drink.)

LISABETTE. Give what?

CASEY. This. I don't have to put up with this hellish life. I have other skills.

HOLLY. Let me guess...

CASEY. For six years I worked in a slaughterhouse.

LISABETTE. No.

CASEY. Yeah.

LISABETTE. No way. You worked in your dad's hardware store.

CASEY. That was earlier. Where's the chocolates?

HOLLY. *(Handing her the box.)* There's only creams left.

CASEY. I took the slaughterhouse job because it paid more than waitressing, and I could cut the pigs' throats at night, which left my days free to audition.

HOLLY. Was there a lot of blood?

CASEY. Gouts.

HOLLY. I hate blood.

LISABETTE. I faint. I fainted the first time I had my period.

CASEY. I mean, look at us. Holly's the Frankenstein monster. You teach third grade. I support myself as a murderess from midnight to dawn so I can do godawful plays for free in black box theatres built into linen closets in welfare hotels. This is a career in the arts in America.

LISABETTE. But now we get to do Chekhov! It's like lacework. It's beautiful and delicate and demands everything. Everything! It's unbearably sweet and sad and painful, just like our lives.

HOLLY. Don't you love her.

CASEY. Plus I get a paycheck so my mother will think acting is actually a job.

LISABETTE. No, but it's Chekhov!

CASEY. As long as it pays the bills.

LISABETTE. That's so cynical.

CASEY. Lisabette, sweetie, I'm not cynical. Look at me. I'm like a beating heart you can hold in your hand. I just happen to live in a country where they give people who do what I do endless shit.

LISABETTE. But why can't it be beautiful? I want it to be beautiful.

CASEY. Lisabette, you're drunk.

LISABETTE. I am, I'm really drunk. But the three of us are so sad, right? I mean, I'm sad because I'm hopelessly naïve and have absolutely no idea what will become of me, like I'm running down the railway tracks and the train is coming. *(To CASEY.)* And you're sad because you're hoping against hope when you really probably know there is no hope. *(To HOLLY.)* And you're sad because... why are you sad, I forget?

HOLLY. I am sad because that beautiful country singer dissed me, and now I'm going to have to make him pay, and that'll make me feel badly about myself, and that'll put me back in therapy which means I have to switch therapists because my last one is too busy writing screenplays.

LISABETTE. See, Chekhov knows us.

CASEY. *(Nodding.)* 'Fraid so.

LISABETTE. To Chekhov.

(There is a knock on the door.)

LISABETTE. Who is it?

KATE. *(Outside.)* Lisabette? It's Kate. Kate Todoravskia. I wondered if you would like to drink red wine with me and make love?

LISABETTE. *(Sotto voice to the sisters.)* Oh my God.

KATE. I find you unbearably beautiful. I can't think, I can't eat. I want to produce *Romeo and Juliet* for you.

LISABETTE. *(To the sisters.)* What do I do?

(HOLLY beckons LISABETTE over and whispers.)

KATE. I just want to hold you. You could move into my apartment. I have a satellite dish.

LISABETTE. Kate?

KATE. *(Still outside.)* Yes?

LISABETTE. It's a little awkward because I'm in here having sex with Holly.

(LISABETTE mouths "Pardon me Jesus" to the ceiling.)

KATE. With Holly?

HOLLY. With Holly.

KATE. Oh... never mind... goodbye.

(They wait as KATE's footsteps recede.)

CASEY. Now that's Chekhov.

LISABETTE. Thank you, thank you, thank you!

HOLLY. No problem.

LISABETTE. *(Turning to CASEY, meaning KATE's crush.)* Did you know that?

(CASEY indicates "yes.")

HOLLY. Hey, Lisabette.

LISABETTE. What?

HOLLY. In my world, you'd be right there looking at her satellite dish.

(A change now moves from the apartment to a circle of folding chairs. It takes place during the opening half of KATE's speech.)

KATE. Dearest friends. Dearest, dearest actors. You may wonder why at this our first rehearsal I have spoken of my childhood for three hours. Why, I have told you of my Mother, the only American killed by prairie dogs, of my Father whose love of literature inspired him to inscribe 3 chapters of Tolstoy's *War and Peace* on the convex side of a single contact lens which was then tragically lost at Daytona Beach. These then are the threads with which I wove my love of the Russian Classics, and then carried in my heart here to San Antonio... San Antonio is to Houston as rural Russia is to Moscow. The sisters of San Antonio, their hearts beat with this play. We know what it is to be isolated, vulgarized, *we know* what it is to work! This play runs in our veins. Its pain is our pain. The pain of the women of San Antonio. So I say to you, on the brink of rehearsal, the final lines of Chekhov's Texas play, *The Three Sisters,* "In a little while we shall know why we live and why we suffer!"

(Applause from those gathered.)

CASEY. But that's not the final line, right?

KATE. I was speaking metaphorically.

CASEY. Because the final line is, "If only we knew."

KATE. Yes, Casey, that is the final line. Thank you.

CASEY. Said twice.

KATE. I'd like to move on if that's all right?

CASEY. Hey, it's your theatre.

KATE. Thank you. Thank you. And now it is my extraordinary pleasure to introduce our fabulous director, Wikéwitch Konalkvis, a fellow Pole and recent émigré who has directed 71 Chekhov productions and...

WIKÉWITCH. Seventy-two.

KATE. ... 72 productions and...

WIKÉWITCH. No, you are right, 71.

KATE, ... 71 productions and...

WIKÉWITCH. Every one jewel. Make beating heart of Chekhov.

KATE. ... and I just want to say...

WIKÉWITCH. Make beautiful from the pain of love this life which is like some...

KATE. ... he is *so*...

WIKÉWITCH. You, I know, will play Olga. You have pain. Have loss. Radiating of loss. Good. Good Olga.

KATE. I just want to say, and I'm likely to get a little emotional ...

HOLLY. Could we go around the room and meet the other actors?

KATE. Oh.

HOLLY. So we like know who we are. Like we were beginning a *process.*

KATE. Absolutely.

HOLLY. Holly Seabé, which probably goes without saying, Masha.

CASEY. Casey Mulgraw, radiating of loss, Olga.

LISABETTE. Lisabette Cartwright, Irina.

(Now T-ANNE moves from chair to chair, being all the other actors.)

GUNTER. Gunter Sinsel, Solyony.

ALLEN. Allen Greif, thrilled to be Andrey.

JAMES. James George, the hapless Tusenbach.

WIKÉWITCH. *(Ferocious.)* Not hapless!

JAMES. The definitely-not-hapless Tusenbach.

(T-ANNE indicates it would take too much time to do every introduction.)

T-ANNE. *(On book.)* Talk, talk, talk, talk, talk, talk, talk, talk, talk. Introductions over.

WIKÉWITCH. Okay, now I talk...

KATE. Could I...

WIKÉWITCH. You are going to speak of deep love you feel for Chekhov...

KATE. Yes, because when I was 15...

WIKÉWITCH. Stop! This love for Chekhov is like American fantasy. You make God from Chekhov. You say Chekhov, bullshit, Chekhov, bullshit, Chekhov, bullshit, bullshit, bullshit. From God we can't make play. From God we make worship. Worship makes boring play. You want to know in this room who is God? Who is God here?

LISABETTE. *(A guess.)* You are?

WIKÉWITCH. This is very intelligent young actress. God in theatre is interpretation of play. I, Wikéwitch, make interpretation... In this room, in this time, I, Wikéwitch, will be God.

JOBY. Excuse me.

WIKÉWITCH. This is audience. Audience is talking!

JOBY. I mean, this is driving me crazy! This is the whole problem with 20th century theatre. This is part of the reason nobody wants to buy a ticket. We used to get stories; now we get "interpretations." The director is not God!

WIKÉWITCH. I am God.

JOBY. You are not God!

CASEY. Joby...

JOBY. *What*?!

CASEY. A character is talking.

JOBY. I know a character is talking, so?

CASEY. Who says it's the author's view?

WIKÉWITCH. *(Triumphantly.)* You are making interpretation!

JOBY. I don't care whose view it is, it's pernicious.

WIKÉWITCH. You are being God. Who gave you this position?

JOBY. I have a ticket!

WIKÉWITCH. If I do not make interpretation, you cannot make interpretation of my interpretation. You are secondary! I am artist! I fuck you with my art and you cry out.

JOBY. What the hell are you talking about?

WIKÉWITCH. Sit down, little audience, I give you *Three Sisters*. From big soul.

CASEY. *(Trying to calm her.)* Joby...

JOBY. I have never heard such unadulterated...

CASEY. Joby...

JOBY. Sit here and listen to...

CASEY. Joby! *(JOBY stops talking.)* Not now.

JOBY. Then "now" what?

CASEY. You are the audience, Joby. If you talk to us all the time, you become an actor, and then you would have to come down here. Do you want to come down here?

(JOBY, still upset, stands in silence for a moment, then, making a decision, sits back down. DON BLOUNT enters.)

KATE. Don!

DON. Running a little late.

KATE. Don Blount, everybody, Vice President for Grants and Contributions at Albert & Sons Tobacco, our wonderful corporate sponsor.

DON. Don't mean to interrupt. Please go on with the Art.

KATE. Thanks Don. Now, we have the opportunity to make Chekhov with... *(Indicating WIKÉWITCH.)* this fine artist...

WIKÉWITCH. Great artist.

KATE. Great artist, and I feel deeply, even profoundly, that...

DON. *(Back in the scene.)* Could I just say a couple of things...

(DON taps watch.)

WIKÉWITCH. Okay. I pee now.

DON. ... because, uh... well, I'm not part of your world... I'm a businessman. I actually have things to do.

KATE. Oh, Don, absolutely. Don Blount, everybody. Our underwriter.

DON. This is really a... revelation... for me to get to see what art's really all about. It's just that, uh... *(Taps watch.)* So I wanted to say that Albert & Sons Tobacco is really pleased to make this gift to the community of... *Four Sisters... (CASEY holds up three fingers.) Three Sisters.* Sorry. Because Albert & Sons Tobacco International... we're in 130 countries, but we feel our role in this community is to...

CASEY. Kill people.

DON. Excuse me.

CASEY. Your role is to kill people, to target children and African Americans and to seek profit independent of any ethics or morality.

KATE. Oh dear.

CASEY. And by involving yourself in the arts who have no money and have no alternative to taking your minuscule handout, you hope to give the impression that you are on the side of life, when actually you are merchants of death.

DON. *(Pause.)* Thank you so much for the feedback. Albert & Sons respects others and their disparate and useful points of view. But in closing, I will say to you personally that if you take money from us it is disingenuous to make a pretense of morality and that historically, insofar as I understand it, actors were traditionally pickpockets, whores, and parasites on the body politic. Of course, given that your very profession is pretense, I still have the pleasure of enjoying your morality as entertainment. *(Taps watch.)* Got to go. Good luck with however many sisters you've got.

(DON leaves. There is a stunned moment. Lights down)

END OF ACT I

ACT II

(The act opens with a bare stage, one folding chair and an inch-high, two-foot square box that HOLLY stands on while being fitted for her dress as MASHA.)

JACKEY. *(The Costume designer.)* Baby-Darlin'-honey-dear, your luscious body is a costume designer's dream ! You have proportions goin' on like Greek statuary on a good day! Oh, my goodness! Your "out arm center back to wrist bent" is a world-class pisser. Your "shoulder point to mid-bust to center waist" is to die for, and your "depth of crotch and nipple to nipple" would turn Cleopatra mauve with envy. Golly-good-ness-gracious, darlin', you are Masha the bomb!

HOLLY. But this is like, "Why have a body?"

JACKEY. Well, a little draggy, but 1901, if you see what I mean?

HOLLY. I am not going out there dressed up like a funeral cake. This would be, in fact, a good dress for somebody ugly. I mean, Olga might look like this, sure.

JACKEY. Au contraire, my goddess, au contraire. Every man in that audience is gonna hafta keep his program over his lap.

HOLLY. Ugly does not enhance luscious. People who wear ugly become ugly. Are we trying to make me ugly? I am not here to suffer the revenge of the ugly Texans. And I am not beautiful in this dress!

(WIKÉWITCH enters.)

WIKÉWITCH. Okay, okay. So. Masha is great beauty, yes?
But is hiding. Hide-and-go-seek-Masha.

HOLLY. The west coast, we don't hide it. All right, a slit—
waist to floor—let a little leg out.

JACKEY. 1901, honeydoll, no tits, no slits.

WIKÉWITCH. Repress. Very constrict. Very dark. This is
sex for brain peoples.

HOLLY. Brain peoples. Reality check, all right?

JACKEY. *(Working.)* Ooooo, reality, I don't live there.

HOLLY. I spent $114,000 on my legs. I was in rehab for
three months with animal, killer, monster rehab nurses in the
Dominican Republic. An Internet survey shows that my legs
alone, without the rest of me, have 19 million fans. I either
have legs or I walk. *(JACKEY has his head in his hands.)*
Jackey, will you stop crying. Every time we have a fitting,
you weep.

JACKEY. You think I want to make women ugly because
I'm a gay man.

HOLLY. Oh, please.

JACKEY. You think I'm hostile because you make mil-
lions, and I do consignment store windows.

HOLLY. Okay, all right, I'm going to try something completely new for me. I'm going to try compromise.

WIKÉWITCH. No compromise.

JACKEY. I *love* compromise.

HOLLY. Everybody listening? Floor length/see-thru.

WIKÉWITCH. I am in madhouse.

JACKEY. Well, lil' darlin', you would look delicious, but I
keep rememberin' what you said the day you got here as to
how the play was about like a tidal wave of vulgarity sweepin'
everything good and beautiful away, which just made me bawl
like a baby, and how the vulgarity of the rich was not to see the

desperate need of the poor, and how the vulgarity of the poor was to be blind to beauty, and the vulgarity of the intellectual was to separate thought from action. So that everyone in the play was as different as they could be but in this funny way they all shared the same despair.

HOLLY. When did I say that?

JACKEY. Well, it was such a pretty thought, you are such a talk-diva, baby love. But it made me think maybe Masha could be this little simplicity in the sea of vulgarity and get all the attention, an' reviews, an' applause, applause, applause.

HOLLY. Well, if I said that, that's what we should do.

WIKÉWITCH. (To JACKEY.) You are God in other form.

JACKEY. *(Sweetly.)* Well, she said.

HOLLY. No more talking!!! The dress rocks. I gotta book to make rehearsal.

(The scene now transitions into rehearsal. At first we see only the director because HOLLY has a costume change.)

WIKÉWITCH. Okay. Okay. Please stopping. Good. Okay. Leave brain. Brain no more. Brain outside, art inside. What you are doing in this time? Hah? Okay, good. Is very clear, is very smart, is very beautiful, is very *professional*. But is not *art*. No more professional. No good to Chekhov, this professional. No, no, no, no, no, no, no! Peel off skin. Rip open body. Lungs, liver, spleen. Okay. Begin.

HOLLY/MASHA. "I don't know. I don't know. Of course, being used to something means a lot. For example...

WIKÉWITCH. *(Interrupting.)* You say line.

HOLLY/MASHA. *(Confused.)* I did.

WIKÉWITCH. Yes, you *say*, "you don't know."

HOLLY/MASHA. I know the line.

WIKÉWITCH. You don't know!

HOLLY/MASHA. I just said it!

WIKÉWITCH. Saying is not being.

HOLLY. What are you talking about?

WIKÉWITCH. Look, little television actress, Masha say, "I don't know," but you don't know what this is not to know, so you just say line. So this little thing, this "I don't know" is dead, and more you say, you go from corpse to corpse over this dead Chekhov. You make graveyard of scene by just say lines. No good. Okay. Her father, military man, is dead. Real corpse, not acting corpse. Since that moment, this Masha lives, imbeciles all around, peasant idiots, animals, mud, stupidity. Peasant thirsty for drink, they spit in hand, like spit for drink. Only soldiers, like father, have brain. She is thirsty for brain. She says soldiers honorable, educated, worthwhile. Vershinin is soldier. His soul is dead. He knows soldier is animal too. He says this. How can she bear this. This is break her heart. He says this before scene. It is like stone. Like stone. You understand? She says, "I don't know." Yes! This is heart bleeding. Yes! Now you say.

HOLLY. I don't know.

WIKÉWITCH. No.

HOLLY. I don't know.

WIKÉWITCH. No!

HOLLY. What the hell do you want?

WIKÉWITCH. I want you to *be* line, not *say* line!

HOLLY. I don't know!

WIKÉWITCH. No.

HOLLY. I don't know.

WIKÉWITCH. No!

HOLLY. You think I know what the hell you mean but I'm telling you *I don't know*!

WIKÉWITCH. Yes! *Now* you know!

HOLLY. What?!

WIKÉWITCH. What you don't know! Chekhov is back from dead!

(A pause.)

HOLLY. Okay, I get it.
WIKÉWITCH. You get it.
HOLLY. Yes.
WIKÉWITCH. One line. Twenty minutes. You get one scene, I'm dead from old age.
HOLLY. I really get it.
WIKÉWITCH. Enough. Rehearse. Say "I don't know."
HOLLY. I don't know.
WIKÉWITCH. Okay. Next line.

(There are now a series of short BEN/HOLLY scenes with minimal furniture being brought in and out during a continuous flow.)

BEN. Hey.
HOLLY. Hi.
BEN. Ummmm.
HOLLY. Ummmmm?
BEN. Coffee?
HOLLY. Sure.

(Chairs are placed under them and a table between them.)

BEN. I held that kiss too long.
HOLLY. I noticed.
BEN. That was unprofessional.
HOLLY. Nice tongue, though.
BEN. Ma'am, I never meant...
HOLLY. You did.
BEN. I have to go.

(BEN moves away from the table.)

HOLLY. Ben?
BEN. Yeah?
HOLLY. You kiss your wife like that?

(They meet outside rehearsal.)

HOLLY. What the hell's going on in rehearsal?
BEN. Please don't call me at home.
HOLLY. When we're doing the scene, don't avoid the kiss and then say "kiss—kiss over." I feel like I'm in middle school.
BEN. That scene is driving me crazy.
HOLLY. Why is that?
BEN. You know perfectly well why.
HOLLY. Yeah. I do.
BEN. I am married. I have two kids.
HOLLY. I have a live-in lover.
BEN. My wife is ill.
HOLLY. My lover's an ex-convict.
BEN. The kids are waiting for me to come.
HOLLY. Me too. All right, Ben. Come over in the morning. *(A rolling door moves on. BEN knocks. HOLLY opens it. He steps in and immediately kisses her. They start ripping off clothes. Dialogue along this vein ensues.)* My neck. Yes. Yes! My mouth.
BEN. Oh God.
HOLLY. *(While being kissed, she is trying to undo his belt.)* Belt.
BEN. Belt.

(HOLLY keeps trying.)

HOLLY. Can't. Ouch. Hate that belt.

(HOLLY steps back and takes her blouse off over her head. He is working on the belt.)

BEN. Beautiful. Goddamnit, you're beautiful!

HOLLY. I know. *(Trying to undo his buttons.)* Hate these buttons.

BEN. Boots.

HOLLY. *(Pulling his pants down.)* Screw the boots!

JOBY. Excuse me.

BEN. *(Freezes. Pants around his ankles.)* Yes, Joby, we've missed you.

JOBY. I don't think this love story is necessary.

HOLLY. Does anybody have any Tylenol?

(T-ANNE brings her some.)

BEN. The Ben/Holly relationship is a crucial parallel to Masha and Vershinin in *The Three Sisters.*

JOBY. I never read *The Three Sisters.*

HOLLY. Shut up. I'm a character, and you're a character, and I'm cutting your character's lines!

(BEN kisses HOLLY more roughly. They freeze. The lights change. It's now post-coital. BEN pulls up his pants.)

BEN. You were incredible.

HOLLY. Lots of practice.

BEN. What in the hell did you say that for?

HOLLY. Because it's true. It doesn't mean I didn't like it.

BEN. I'm not kidding around here, Holly.

HOLLY. Okay. It was my first time.

(The scene breaks up. Two period chairs and a standing lamp become the set for rehearsal.)

HOLLY/MASHA. What a noise the stove's making. The wind was... line?

T-ANNE. *(Prompting.)* Moaning in the chimney.

HOLLY/MASHA. ... moaning in the chimney just before Father died.

T-ANNE. The same sound exactly.

HOLLY/MASHA. The same sound exactly.

BEN/VERSHININ. Are you superstitious?

HOLLY/MASHA. Yes.

BEN/VERSHININ. Strange. *(Kisses her hand.)* You magnificent, magical woman. Magnificent, magical! It's dark in here but I can see the shining of your eyes.

HOLLY/MASHA. There's more light over here...

BEN/VERSHININ. I'm in love, I'm in love, I'm in love...

(BEN/VERSHININ stops.)

T-ANNE. *(Prompting.)* In love with your eyes, with the way you move.

BEN. *(Out of scene.)* I don't want to do this.

HOLLY. *(Out of scene.)* Are you?

BEN. Am I what?

HOLLY. In love?

T-ANNE. *(Prompting.)* In love with your eyes, with...

HOLLY. Can it, okay? You are or you aren't.

BEN. I have a real life. I can hurt real people here.

HOLLY. And what am I, animation? You think I'm not susceptible? Hey, man, three years ago, I'm involved with a guy commits suicide jumping off the Golden Gate Bridge in a wedding dress. Two years ago, the guy I'm living with whacks me, breaks my jaw so I couldn't work for three weeks and they almost pulled the show. Right now, as we speak, my significant other is an actor who has an immobilizing drinking problem mainly because in high school he murdered his prom date and served eleven years. You see why I might be susceptible to some ordinary, straight-up guy? Okay, it's mutual.

(Lights come up on JOBY. HOLLY sees it.)

JOBY. Excuse me.
HOLLY. Don't even think about it!

(HOLLY leaves. Furniture is struck. An exercycle and some mats become the gym.)

CASEY. So, the casting agent says to me, "You're not right for it; you're a character woman." I die. My blood congeals. Fissures appear. It's the actresses' death knell. I go through menopause in five seconds. All fluids dry. I become the Mojave Desert. Character woman! I, who have screwed every leading man on the East Coast, become their mother. Vertigo. I scream out in a silent, unattending universe: "I'm too young to be a character woman!" and the echo replies, rolling out of infinite space: "They want to see you for the funny aunt at the wedding!"

(CASEY ritually disembowels herself. HOLLY enters in exercise clothes. All three begin to work out; HOLLY particularly exercises fiercely.)

CASEY. Bad day?
HOLLY. Bad day.
LISABETTE. Bad day.
CASEY: Bad day. *(They exercise.)* Why does every actor in America go to the gym?
HOLLY. Because it's a beauty contest, not a profession.

(They exercise.)

LISABETTE. Damn it to hell! *(She drops the weights.)* Wikéwitch called me dense as a turkey, an' I'm a lot smarter than a turkey. An' then he picked on me for three hours an' I cried an' he patted me on my shoulder an' I threw up all over him. Then I ran out an' tripped over the doorjamb an' cracked a tooth an' I could just spit fire an' eat broke glass.

CASEY. *(Exercising.)* He called you a turkey?

LISABETTE. He didn't call me a turkey. He said I had the brain of a turkey.

HOLLY. Wikéwitch is a tyrannical, woman-hating buttwipe, but he seems to know what he's doing. *(They exercise.)* Meanwhile, my boyfriend has just been arrested for sexually soliciting a seven-foot transsexual on Hollywood Blvd. who turned out to be a policewoman on stilts, so *People* magazine called me for a quote.

(They exercise.)

CASEY. What'd you say?

HOLLY. I said it just showed he missed me.

(They exercise.)

CASEY. Play's going pretty well. *(They exercise.)* Whattayathink? *(They exercise.)* Play's going pretty well.

HOLLY. I wouldn't know, I've never done a play.

(CASEY and LISABETTE stop exercising.)

CASEY. You are kidding? Are you kidding?

HOLLY. From high school on TV... well, I was in one play, but I had to leave to get an abortion. One play and one porn flic.

LISABETTE. You didn't do a porn flic!?

HOLLY. *(Still exercising.)* Yeah.

CASEY. Tell.

HOLLY. Actually I got fired.

LISABETTE. How do you get fired from a porn flic?

HOLLY. I came. Joking. I got fired because I started crying uncontrollably on camera. It depressed the porn divas so they dumped me.

LISABETTE. Why were you crying?

HOLLY. Because I came. First time. Consider those implications.

(They all exercise.)

LISABETTE. What if it were good?

CASEY. What?

LISABETTE. You know.

CASEY. Our little Russian skit? The Sisters Three?

LISABETTE. I mean, what if it were *really* good? Really. Really, really good. Could we? You're good. You're both good. We could do something good. Could we do something good? It could be good. It could be really, really good. Could it? Be good?

CASEY. I once believed I could be very good. I wanted to be so concentrated, so compressed, so vivid and present and skillful and heartfelt that anyone watching me would literally burst into flame. Combust.

LISABETTE. That *kills* me. I *want* that. Did you ever do it? Did it ever happen?

CASEY. No.

LISABETTE. But maybe we could do that? What would happen if we did that?

HOLLY. Nobody would care.

LISABETTE. That's so cold. How can you say that? It could change people's lives.

CASEY. God love you, Lisabette, two months later the **audience can't remember the name of the play.**

LISABETTE. *I don't believe that. I don't believe that.*

CASEY. Has anybody you know to be a sentient being ever walked up to you and said the play changed their life? No, fine, okay. You know who is changed by Chekhov? Me. I finish a play, it's like, "Get me an exorcist!" He eats my life. He chews me up. He spits me out. I'm like bleeding from Chekhov. The audience? Who knows what their deal is? They come from the mists; they return to the mist. They cough, they sneeze, they sleep, they unwrap little hard candies, and then they head for their cars *during* the curtain call. And once, once I would like to step out and say to the ones who are up the aisles while we take the bows, "Hey! Excuse me! Could you show a little mercy because I just left it all out here on the stage and even if you don't have the foggiest notion what it was or what it meant, could you have the common courtesy to leave your goddamn cars in the garage for another 40 seconds and give me a little hand for twenty years of work!

JOBY. That is unmitigated hogwash.

HOLLY. Oh, please...

JOBY. I don't cough or sleep or unwrap little candies, I come to feel. *(She taps her head and chest.)* Here and here. Because if I'm ever going to understand my own life, it will have to be through feeling, and my own life and experience isn't big enough so I come for enlargement. Plus I want the highest quality moments for my life I can get, and you're supposed to provide them, though you usually don't, so when I write my review...

CASEY. Hold it.

JOBY ... I need to point out whether there is any enlargement...

HOLLY. Your review?

JOBY ... to be had by the audience...

CASEY. You're a critic.

JOBY. ... in this particular experience!

CASEY. You have been interrupting us all night...

JOBY. I am part of the process.

CASEY. After the play, not *during* the play.

JOBY. After the play I'm not part of the process. After the play you revile and dismiss me. Some of you claim you don't even read reviews which is a complete joke!

CASEY. I don't read reviews.

JOBY. You do.

CASEY. Don't.

JOBY. Do.

CASEY. Don't.

JOBY. Do.

CASEY. Okay, sometimes.

JOBY. Hah!

CASEY. Look, we only put up with you because half our audience is three months from the nursing home.

HOLLY. I can't believe it—a critic!?

JOBY. Well...

HOLLY. How are we doing so far?

JOBY. Well, it's definitely interesting, sometimes amusing, well paced, but a very uneasy mix of...

LISABETTE. Stop! Not while we're doing it! Critics are gods to me. I completely measure my self-worth by my reviews.

HOLLY. Who do you write for?

JOBY. *(A pause.)* I don't want to talk about it.

(JOBY sits down.)

CASEY. That is completely unfair. We have to go on here. Do we have to be afraid of you or not?

JOBY. It doesn't matter who I write for; it matters what I perceive.

CASEY. Joby, even you don't believe that. Don't tell me there isn't a critical hierarchy when you would poison your colleagues for the six best jobs.

JOBY. Not my job.

CASEY. *Who do you write for*, Joby?

JOBY. *Bargain Mart Suburban Shoppers Guide.*

CASEY. *(Turning back to the stage.)* She's nobody, let's act.

JOBY. I am *not* nobody!

CASEY. *(Referring back.)* I didn't mean you personally, Joby.

(JOBY sits down. The actresses exercise.)

LISABETTE. What was wrong with your day, Casey?

CASEY. Forget it.

LISABETTE. We told you.

CASEY. Forget it.

LISABETTE. We're not important enough to tell?

(They exercise a moment in silence.)

CASEY. I felt a lump in the shower. I saw a doctor. She wants to do a biopsy.

HOLLY. When?

CASEY. On the day off.

LISABETTE. Oh my God.

(CASEY exercises. LISABETTE is frozen. HOLLY stops exercising, stands and walks over to CASEY, who keeps working out.)

HOLLY. *(Standing above her.)* Stop. *(CASEY does. HOLLY puts out her hand.)* Get off. *(CASEY does.)* Hug me.

(CASEY does.)

BEN. Excuse me?
LISABETTE. Yes?
BEN. It's Ben.
HOLLY. Come in.

(BEN does.)

BEN. I left my wife.

(A moment.)

CASEY. Well, either way I lose my hair.

(HOLLY and CASEY exit. The gym is struck and a desk and two chairs are brought on for DON BLOUNT's office.)

DON. Don Blount of Albert & Sons Tobacco calling for Martha Graham. Then why is it called the Martha Graham Dance Company? Oh. No, I knew that. Little joke. Listen, the grant's in the mail. Yes. Well, it's our pleasure to support a dance company of your caliber and if you might find an opportunity to mention to the chairman of your board that we'd be thrilled if she'd tell her brother the congressman to stop sodomizing the tobacco industry just because he's personally in the pocket of the HMO's, I think you'd find your grant is definitely renewable. My pleasure. *(DON hangs up the phone, picks it back up and dials.)* Mom, it's Don. Your son Don. I need the favor, Mom. I know we did it yesterday, but I'm feeling a little alienated... a little remote. Wonderful. Good. I knew I could count on you, Momma. Ready? All right, light it up, Mom. Inhale, Mom. Would I encourage you to smoke if there was any danger? That's right, I wouldn't. I would never harm my mom. I must be a good person if I would never harm my mom. If I'm a good person, it must be all right to do what I do. Thanks, I feel a lot better. Put it out now, Momma. Everything's all right. I feel damn good. Go back on the oxygen, Ma. See you Sunday.

(KATE enters Albert & Sons. DON rises, smiling and affable.)

DON. Ms. Todoravskia, it's really nice of you to come over on short notice.

KATE. No, I've been wanting to...

DON. Can I get you something?

KATE. Well...

DON. At this level in the executive suite, we could fly in crab's legs from Iceland. Just kidding. But in Iceland the crabs have pneumonia. Wouldn't affect their legs though. Just kidding. Tea, coffee, soft drink, bottled water, mixed drinks of all kinds, munchies, brownies my mother sends in... *(Does his Dracula imitation.)* Cigarette?!

KATE. No, I...

DON. You know, Kate... may I call you Kate? Nice dress, by the way. I deal with a lot of artists, and usually they look like they bought their clothes from the llama shop in Costa Rica.

KATE. Well, I...

DON. I can't tell you how impressed I was by that rehearsal of whatsit you let me see.

KATE. *Three Sisters.*

DON. Well, it just seemed like a metaphor for the lives we all lead, don't you think?

KATE. Well I...

DON. Plus it confirmed my every doubt about corporate investment in Russia. In that way it was very personal for me.

KATE. I'm glad that you...

DON. So it's a real downer to have to pull the funding. Oh, I think we also have fruit juices.

KATE. The funding.

DON . The funding. In a way here, Ms. Todoravskia, I have to tell you I personally blew it. I've only been in Grants and Contributions with Albert & Sons for a couple of months—before that, they let me do real work—just kidding, and I didn't realize when I gave you the okay that there had been a policy change up top.

KATE. Do you mean...

DON. Let me just wrap this up and then we'll relate. We had sort of turned our contribution policy on a dime based on the fact that all this tobacco legislation, politically motivated lawsuits, advertising restrictions have made it clear to us that our market focus in the future will be overseas where they just plain old like a good smoke. Plus their life expectancy is so low that we don't really constitute a health hazard. Hah! Just kidding. Just kidding. And it's in those communities in our target market we'll be looking to leverage our contributions. So the bad news is that I didn't have the authority to give you the money. I hope this won't inconvenience you?

KATE. But you did authorize it.

DON. *(Smiling.)* Poof.

KATE. But we're in the middle of the work.

DON. Poof.

KATE. We will have to default on the salaries and the Board will fire me.

DON. You know, I'm very interested in artists and how they function, and a little research shows an overwhelming percentage of the best work didn't have grants. As far as I can see, good art is almost invariably a product of good old-fashioned adversity and rage. Anger is the engine of art, so in an odd way this is a good situation for you. You don't want to be the lap dog of big tobacco. We're the bad guys. Great art is a personal passion, not a grant. Ms. Todoravskia, Albert & Sons Tobacco is sorry to defund you, but that doesn't mean we aren't proud to fuel your anger.

KATE. I cannot believe...

DON. I'm afraid that's all the time I have for you. I do

however want to make a $75 personal contribution to your theatre. If you wonder about the cost basis, it's the same amount I give to public radio, which I actually use. *(She takes the envelope. He heads back for his desk.)* Oh, listen, I wonder if you have Holly Seabé's phone number?

(Office is struck. The girls are talking—one seated. KATE enters with her suitcase.)

KATE. Hi.

(KATE puts down her suitcase.)

LISABETTE. Hi.
CASEY. Hi.
HOLLY. Hi.
KATE. I, uh... are my eyes red? *(Furious.)* I hate it when my eyes are red!! Sorry, I'm sorry. Look, I want to... uh... tell you how proud... proud I am of you... *(She pauses on the brink of something. It explodes.)* To hell with everybody!! Okay, that feels better... umm, it was very emotional to see this great play being so well done in our little theatre that has... struggled and... held on by its fingernails... *believe me...* for all these years. When I settled here, having attended Stanford, Harvard and Yale, I hoped... I *hoped*!!.. well, those rehearsals were what I hoped for as an artist. They surpassed my hopes. It's one hell of a time to be fired, I'll tell you that.

LISABETTE. Oh my God...

KATE. Albert & Sons removed the funding.

CASEY. Oh God.

KATE. And when I told Joe Bob Mattingly, the Chairman of our Board of Directors, he said...

JOE BOB. *(From somewhere out in the house.)* Damn woman! You got no more sense than a hog on ice! I been pourin' my money an' the money of my friends down your double-talk rathole since Jesus was a pup, so my wife could drag me down here to see plays nobody can understand with a buncha people I would never invite to dinner, on the basis it creates some quality of life I'm supposed to have since I figgered out how to make some money. Half the time, that stuff doesn't have a story, and it's been five years since you done one takes place in a kitchen, which is the kind all of us like. The rest of the time it's about how rich people is bad and Democrats is good and white people is stupid and homosexuals have more fun an' we should get rid of the corporations an' eat grass an' then, by God, you wonder why you don't have a big audience! Now you just blew 15% of your budget 'cause you riled up the tobacco interests, plus you got the colored rattlin' on my cage, and as of this precise minute, you are out of luck, out of work an outta San Antonio, Texas. See, I am closin' us down, lockin' the door, an' then, by God, we can go back to hittin' each other up to give to the United Way where it will, by God, do some poor handicap some actual, measurable good, an' I won't have to hear anybody say "aesthetic" from one year to the goddamned next! Now, vaya con Dios, darlin'.

JOE BOB and KATE. You got three minutes to clean out your desk.

(JOE BOB disappears. KATE speaks to CASEY.)

KATE. So that's it. They said if I was out of the city before five o'clock I'd get six months' severance and my plane ticket. What, do you suppose, I thought I was doing here? Making theatre because... See I just can't remember. Well, I guess nobody told us everything has a purpose.

CASEY. Man cannot live by bread alone.

KATE. No, he needs salsa. *(Shakes CASEY's hand.)* Actually, I think I hate theatre. It makes you think it was about something when it was actually only about yourself. It fascinates you. It seduces you. It leaves you penniless by the side of the road. Screw Thespis! *(She looks at the women.)* Run for your lives.

(KATE exits. The women look at each other.)

LISABETTE. Goodness gracious.

(LISABETTE wipes tear.)

CASEY. You okay?
LISABETTE. I guess.
JOBY. *(From audience.)* Don't let it get too sentimental.
CASEY. *(Without looking up.)* Thanks for the tip. *(Turns to HOLLY.)* So that this doesn't get too sentimental, why don't you pay for the production? You have the money.
HOLLY. Why would I do that?
CASEY. Self-interest?
HOLLY. Ah.
CASEY. You want the credit. You don't like to be pushed around. You're secretly thrilled you're good in the part. Based on proving you can act, you might get a film where you kept your clothes on. And I could use the distraction from the fact the biopsy was positive.
HOLLY. That's not too sentimental. Anything else?
CASEY. No, that's about it.
HOLLY. *(Seeing BEN enter.)* Hi.
BEN. Stay.
HOLLY. *(Turns to LISABETTE.)* And you, little one?
LISABETTE. It might make you happy.

(HOLLY chuckles.)

HOLLY. Well, that aside, why not?
CASEY. You'll pay to get us open?
HOLLY. I'll get us open.
LISABETTE. No way?
HOLLY. They screwed with us, now they lose.
LISABETTE. You really mean it?
HOLLY. I don't want to talk about it, I want to do it.

(At this point WIKÉWITCH walks in with his suitcase.)

WIKÉWITCH. So. Is not to be. Okay. I put life in small suitcase. You. You. You. On we go, yes? Is hard to tell what is good, what is bad. Everything is doorway to something else. *(Shaking hands.)* Little Irina, okay, goodbye. Olga. Olga, she goes on. Vershinin. He finds another girl next town. *(To HOLLY.)* Like cat you land on feet, yes?
CASEY. It's not over.
WIKÉWITCH. No?
CASEY. We have the money. We can open.
WIKÉWITCH. Where is money?
HOLLY. Here is money.
WIKÉWITCH. Ah. Is for what?
LISABETTE. So we can do your beautiful play.
WIKÉWITCH. Ah. Okay, okay. Honorable sisters and Lieutenant Colonel. Okay. I wake, wake, wake. No sleeping. Okay. I get up, pack suitcase, close suitcase. Knock, knock, knock. Theatre producer says no more money. Dead Chekhov. Okay. Bye-bye. Money, money, money. But, dear American actors, before knock-knock, I am pack. So why is this? Because work is finish. When do Chekhov, now, now, now, young, middle, old. So much you can do, only what you know. No more. Then wait for life to teach. You are sweet young people, but what I know... *(Points to head.)* ... you cannot do. What for I do this? No sleep, no sleep. We must be a little realistic in this time.

For you, Chekhov is fantasy. For me, life. You have nice, small talent. We can do together baby-Chekhov. Okay, *but* I have... short time... short time now... no sleep... no time for baby-Chekhov... I must take small suitcase, find big souls to do play, so I don't die with this Chekhov in my head. This you understand or not understand?

HOLLY. We're not good enough.

WIKÉWITCH. You do not understand. OK. Bye-bye. *(Goes to exit and turns back.)* You are good enough to do the Chekhov you are good enough to do. But is not good enough.

(WIKÉWITCH tips his hat and is gone.)

LISABETTE. See, I've always been terrified that some guy dressed in black would show up and tell me I'm not good enough.

HOLLY. Yeah, but what he said was:

CASEY and HOLLY. You just have to do the Chekhov you're good enough to do.

LISABETTE. He did say that.

HOLLY. Okay. We'll do the Chekhov we can do.

LISABETTE. Really?

HOLLY. Really.

LISABETTE. Yes! Oh yes! *(To CASEY.)* Can you believe this? Can we please work on the last scene? *(She picks up the script.)* I want to work on the last scene.

HOLLY. Where from?

LISABETTE. The band. Ta ra ra boom de ay.

CASEY. We're over here.

HOLLY/MASHA. "Oh, but listen to the band! They're leaving us."

T-ANNE. *(Entering.)* Sorry. Sorry to interrupt. Phone for you, Holly.

HOLLY. Take the message.

(HOLLY turns back to the scene.)

T-ANNE. Dreamworks.

(A moment.)

HOLLY. *(To the others.)* I'll be right back.

(HOLLY goes.)

LISABETTE. What's Dreamworks?
CASEY. Who are you? What planet do you live on? Spielberg.
LISABETTE. Oh, you mean...
T-ANNE. *(As a stage manager, cutting to another place in the text.)* Talk, talk, talk, talk, talk, talk, talk. Holly comes back.

(HOLLY does.)

HOLLY. I got a film.
CASEY. You are kidding?

(HOLLY shakes her head. No, she's not kidding.)

LISABETTE. That is great! That is so exciting! What is it! I never heard anybody say that, "I got a film." I was right here when you said it!
CASEY. When?
LISABETTE. What when?
CASEY. *(Directly to HOLLY.)* When film?
HOLLY. Now. Yesterday. I'm replacing somebody who walked.
LISABETTE. Now?

HOLLY. They want me on a flight in 90 minutes. Jesus, I gotta pack. Rental car? How will I get rid of the rental car? Damn it, my dogs? How the hell am I going to do that? I'm supposed to film tonight.

CASEY. How long?

HOLLY. One month, L.A.; one month, Thailand. I mean, the part is dogmeat. Girlfriend stuff. Two scenes naked, three scenes I listen to the guy talk, once scene I get crushed by pythons. Two months I say a dozen sentences. Listen, I am... I am sorry, I am really sorry, but I am really happy... bad for you, good for me... me, me, me... and I can't even pretend I'm anything but euphoric! Kill me, I'm horrible! Gotta go, gotta go.

(HOLLY starts to race out.)

BEN. I'll come with.

HOLLY. Damn.

BEN. I don't have anything here. I got rid of everything here. You're it.

HOLLY. You just don't have a clue who you got mixed up with, do you?

BEN. I love you.

HOLLY. I got the call. We've just been fooling around while I waited for the call.

BEN. I'll just come out and hang.

HOLLY. Oh Ben. You just don't get it. This is the shot. You are a very sweet cowboy, but it makes you, don't you see, completely disposable, babe. Trust me, you don't want to hang around Malibu while I give head for billing. This is it. I will take no prisoners. You have to blow me off. You know what? *(She kisses his cheek.)* Go back to your wife. Sorry to be the meat grinder. It's just the way it plays out. *(Looks at him.)* I got a couple minutes, tell me to go screw myself. *(He shakes his head.)* Okay. *(She kisses him.)* Bye L. *(Hugs LISABETTE.*

Appraises CASEY.) More I see of you, you could probably get it done for a hundred thousand. *(CASEY chuckles; they hug.)* Anything I can do, you call me. We almost made it, huh?

CASEY. Almost.

HOLLY. I'm no surprise to you guys, I know that. Gotta go. Want to know the really worst part? I-am-so-happy!

(HOLLY leaves.)

CASEY. You okay, Ben?

(BEN nods yes.)

LISABETTE. *(Concerned.)* What will you do?

(BEN shakes his head "I don't know.")

CASEY. She was really beautiful, huh? *(BEN nods yes.)* Kind of like really sexy Russian roulette, right? Only you're alive.

BEN. *(A pained smile.)* Thanks.

(BEN exits.)

LISABETTE. What will we do?
CASEY. When the play's over, you pack.
LISABETTE. I live here.
CASEY. Then I will allow you to skip the packing.
LISABETTE. What will you do?
CASEY. What will I do? Oh, probably get my other breast lopped off, and then I think I will try to accept that you don't necessarily get to do what you want to do. I will try to be a grown-up about that. And after I'm a grown-up, I will try to like doing the things grown-ups like to do. Right now, I'm

thinking hardware store. I am worried, however, that I will make a lousy grown-up and that I will cry a lot and be depressed.

LISABETTE. Oh God.

CASEY. Can I tell you something about theatre?

LISABETTE. Sure.

CASEY. Never ask an out-of-work actress what's next.

LISABETTE. Okay.

CASEY. *(Giving her a hug.)* Pardon you Jesus.

(Chair is struck. An airplane gate table is rolled in, as well as three waiting room chairs that move as a unit. HOLLY enters with luggage.)

AIRPORT ANNOUNCER. Because of weather, the following flights have been canceled or rescheduled: Flight #1726 to Los Angeles, Flight #343 to Dallas/Ft. Worth, Flight #2121 to Seattle, Flight #1643 to San Francisco...

(HOLLY begins talking to a gate check-in person, overlapping the flight cancellations.)

HOLLY. No, you don't understand, I have to be in L.A. by 6 P.M.

GATE MANAGER. Ma'am, we have weather cancellations or long delays on everything going west.

HOLLY. You said that. I am a famous television star who is shooting a movie at 7 P.M. tonight.

GATE MANAGER. Wow, what movie?

HOLLY. Get me on a plane!

GATE MANAGER. Ma'am. Weather is weather, ma'am. There is nothing flying.

HOLLY. *(Overlapping his speech.)* And if I'm not there for the shoot, I will lose the most important job of my career!

GATE MANAGER. I can get you on Flight #1077 arriving L.A. 7:30 A.M. tomorrow.

HOLLY. Too late.

GATE MANAGER. All I've got.

HOLLY. Look, is there a VIP lounge?

GATE MANAGER. Sure.

HOLLY. Is there a sofa in it?

GATE MANAGER. Absolutely.

HOLLY. I'll fuck you for a flight.

GATE MANAGER. You are one sad chick, and I don't have a plane.

HOLLY. *(Apoplectic.)* I'll have your job, do you understand me?!

GATE MANAGER. *(Gently.)* No, you won't, ma'am.

(GATE MANAGER exits.)

HOLLY. *(Utter frustration.)* Arrghrrrahhhhh!

(HOLLY smashes the bag down, kicks it, throws an enraged fit. She then sits with her head in her hands in a row of gate seating. CASEY enters with her bag. LISABETTE tags along.)

CASEY. Holly? *(HOLLY rocks, keening.)* What's the deal?

LISABETTE. Are you okay?

HOLLY. Do I look like I'm okay?

LISABETTE. Oh no, what is it?

CASEY. Holly? *(HOLLY, crying, doesn't look up.)* What's the deal?

LISABETTE. What, what is it?

HOLLY. My flight's canceled, nobody's flying. I called my agent, he says they'll replace me.

LISABETTE. Oh no.

CASEY. You can't connect through another city?

HOLLY. You can't *land* on the West Coast. I'm cursed. It's my karma.

(HOLLY leans on CASEY who now sits beside her.)

LISABETTE. I drove Casey out for her New York flight. We thought we'd check to see if you left.

HOLLY. No, I haven't left! You can't see I haven't left! I can't take this, I can't, I'll kill myself. *(A band is heard in the distance.)* No planes! It's like some incredibly murderous cosmic joke. *(The band's sound intrudes.)* What the hell is that?

CASEY. There's some high school band playing in the terminal.

HOLLY. Does anybody have a goddamn Kleenex? That was my last Kleenex. My life is like a nightmare. I'm a nightmare. *(She blows her nose.)* What happened to Ben?

CASEY. He threw his stuff in his car and drove to Nashville. Said Texas was over, acting was over, his marriage was over and you were over, the end.

HOLLY. Eat me.

(HOLLY puts her head back in her hands. Silence, except for the band. LISABETTE makes the connection with the last scene in The Three Sisters *and sings softly.)*

LISABETTE. Ta-ra-ra boom-de-ay, ta-ra-ra boom-de-ay.
HOLLY. Oh please.

(CASEY wipes at her eyes with another Kleenex.)

LISABETTE. *(Quoting.)* "Let them have their little cry. Doesn't matter, does it?" *(They are in the familiar tableau. HOLLY and LISABETTE sitting, CASEY behind them. She looks at HOLLY.)* Your line.

HOLLY. So?

CASEY. *(A pause.)* It is, it's your line.

HOLLY. Do I give a damn?

CASEY. Yeah, you do.

HOLLY. "Listen. Hear how the band plays. They are leaving us. One has already gone, gone forever, and we are alone, left behind to start life again. We have to live; we must live."

LISABETTE. "A time will come when everyone knows what it was all for and why we suffer. There will be no secrets, but meantime we must live; we must work, only work! Tomorrow I set out alone. I'll teach in a school and give the whole of my own life to those who can make some use of it. Now it's autumn, but winter will come, covering eveything with snow, and I will work; I will work."

CASEY. "The music plays so gaily, vigorously, as if it wants itself to live. Oh, my God. Time will pass, and then we shall be gone forever. They will forget us, our faces, voices, even how many of us there were. But our sufferings will become joy for those who live after us. A season of happiness and peace, and we who lived now will be blessed and thought of kindly. Oh, dear sisters, our life is still not finished. We will live. The music plays so bravely, so joyfully, as if in another moment we shall know why we live and why we suffer. If we could only know, if we could only know!"

(A moment held in the traditional pose, and then CASEY and HOLLY leave the stage. Everyone has gone except LISABETTE. She looks up in the audience and speaks to JOBY.)

LISABETTE. So how did we do?

JOBY. Oh fine. Not bad. Is it over?

LISABETTE. Sort of. I mean I'm the only one left. Their planes left.

JOBY. But not really.

LISABETTE. No, not really. I mean, in the play they left.

JOBY. They don't give me much space in the paper. I'm kind of between the car ads and the pet ads.

LISABETTE. I didn't have a lot of lines either. Not like a lead character or anything.

JOBY. You were good though, with what you had.

LISABETTE. Thanks. And?

JOBY. Oh. Well I... okay umm. So I would say... it played *(The time.),* you know *(The date.),* at *(The place.),* and umm... a seriocomic, ummm, look at the creative drive and how the culture and, like, human frailty warp that, make it less pure... almost ludicrous, maybe breaks it... umm, calls into question whether it's kind of over for the theatre... you know. Pretty good acting and everything... minimal set. I guess my question would be if plays, doing plays, doesn't speak to the culture, then examining why, or satirizing why, is kind of beating a dead horse... from the inside. So, uh, anyway, I only have about a hundred words to say that. You were good.

LISABETTE. Wow.

JOBY. Yeah. I could send you a copy.

LISABETTE. Thanks.

JOBY. I mean, I'm not a real critic... yet.

LISABETTE. Oh, you will be.

JOBY. Yeah. I don't know.

LISABETTE. Really.

JOBY. Yeah. Anyway. Bye.

LISABETTE. Bye.

JOBY. Bye.

(JOBY leaves. Airport is struck. T-ANNE enters and sets a ghost light.)

T-ANNE. 'Night, baby.

LISABETTE. 'Night. *(LISABETTE remains in a single light. She looks around her.)* Wow. Crazy. It's so stupid, but I love to act. It always feels like anything could happen. That something wonderful could happen. It's just people, you know, just people doing it and watching it, but I think everybody hopes that it might turn out to be something more than that. Like people buy a ticket to the lottery, only this has more... heart to it. And most times, it doesn't turn out any better than the lottery, but sometimes... my dad runs a community center, and back in the day they did this play called *Raisin in the Sun,* just about a black family or something, and it was just people doing it. He said there was a grocery guy and a car mechanic, a waitress, but the whole thing had like... I don't know... aura, and people wanted to be there... so much that when they would practice at night, 'cause everybody had jobs, they had to open the doors at the center and hundreds of black people would just show up, show up for the play practice. They brought kids, they brought dinner, old people in wheelchairs, and they would hang around the whole time, kids running up and down, until the actors went home, night after night at practice, and when they finished, these people would stick around and they would line up outside like a... reception line... like a wedding... and the actors would walk down that line... "How you doin'? How you doin'?" shaking hands, pattin' on the kids, and the people would give them pies and yard flowers, and then the audience and the actors would all walk out, in the pitch dark, to the parking lot together. Nobody know exactly what it was or why it happened. Some day I'd like to be in a play like that. I would. So I guess I'll go on... keep trying... what do you think? Could happen. Maybe. Maybe not. *(She looks at the audience.)* Well, you came tonight anyway.

(Blackout.)

END OF PLAY

PROPERTY PLOT

2 Rolling door frames w/door
1 Rolling door w/frame only
14 total folding chair
    A few different colors and styles; used in various scenes
Pad and pen
    For Joby the "critic"

PROLOGUE
Ghost light
    Practical
(Cloak)
    t-anne
SM keys
    t-anne wears
Prompt book
    t-anne/-with blocking
SM table w/dressing
    With: spike tape, stop watch, papers, pencil cups,
    Kleenex, water bottle, chips (eaten nightly)
rolling suitcase
    Lisabette - holds beef jerky and script in front pocket
Tote bag
    Lisabette - has stuff in it
Back pack
    Casey - has actor stuff, script and snickers

AUDITION WAITING ROOM
Beef jerky
    Individually wrapped; not eaten
6 Three Sisters scripts
    Editors versions. 3 same translation, 3 totally different

AUDITION ROOM
Vogue Magazine
   Current
Folding table-seats two
   With: Kleenex box, audition sheets, pencil cups
Squeak markers
   Ralph: audition scene

PHONE MOMS
2 handsets
   Lisabette and Casey

AIRPLANE
2 plane seats
   Coach
2 airplane wine bottles
   The small ones you get on airplanes

1st REHEARSAL/ANDWYNETH
4 xeroxed Three Sisters scripts
   3 highlighted in 2 different colors for the parts of the 3
   sisters
Lipstick
   Applied; in tote
Mirror
   Small, used when lipstick applied
Nail file
   In tote
Skittles
   Eaten nightly
Guitar case
   Ben

PAJAMA PARTY

2 single beds
　　Hote apt. look w/sheets, fully made and castered
4 pillows
　　W/pillow cases
2 chairs
　　in hotel apt.
Box of Kleenex
　　This makes a total of 3; used nightly
Bottle of vodka
　　Probably about 1/2 full
3 glasses
　　Hotel apt. type glasses for the vodka
(sweatshirt)
　　For Casey
Box of chocolates
　　Ala: Russell Stover's w/only the creams left

1st REHEARSAL W/WIKÉWITCH

Briefcase
　　For Don Blount
(watch)
　　For Don Blount

COSTUME FITTING

Cloth tape measure
　　For the costume designer, Jacky
2 clipboards
　　For Jacky and his asst. w/paper and pencils
Box to stand on for fitting
　　Approx. 3" - 4" high

BEN SCENES
2 café chairs
Café table
2 period chairs
  For Three Sisters rehearsal
Standing period lamp
  For Three Sisters rehearsal
Note in sealed envelope
  From Ben to Holly; opened nightly

GYM SCENE
2 exercise mats
Exercise bike
  Modern
2 sets 5 lbs. Gym weights

DON'S OFFICE
Corporate office desk
  Don Blount
Fancy desk chair w/arms
Desk chair
  'For Don's office
Check book & pen
  Check written n ightly
Contribution paper
  Explains contribution policy of Albert & Sons tobacco
Small pan of brownies
  Not eaten
Desk phone
  For Don Blount
Cell phone
  For Don Blount

MEETING
Suitcase
    Kate
Purse
    Kate
Small suitcase
    Wikéwatch

DEPARTURES
Airport counter
    Rolls on, w/keyboard
Airport seating
    Seats three together; rolls on
3 fashionable suitcasre
    Holly; one is a suit bag; they are thrown, kicked, and
    sat upon
Target Suitcase
    Casey; sat upon
Tissues
    For Holly

T-ANNE
Jeans
Grey hoodie
Socks
Backless sneakers
Key chain
Watch
Black cape (for entrance)
Belt?

ANDWYNETH
Sarong (Safety pins)
Black tank top
Black sandals
Red Leather coat
Cowrie earrings
Cowrie necklace
Sunglasses
Rings
Bracelets

DON BLOUNT
Blue striped cotton shirt
Navy two piece suit
Belt
Red tie
Black shoes
Watch
Glasses?
Hairnet?
Socks

EDITOR
Dark gray pants
Dark gray shirt
Black leather jacket
Amber colored glasses
Belt
Black shoes
Socks

KATE
Burgundy dress
Burgundy Coat (Audition
    scene and Goodbye to
    sisters scene)
Dark red heels
Earrings
Necklace
Shawl (First rehearsal
    scene with dress and
    no coat; possibly for
    p.j. party scene)
Scarf (Don Blount's ofc.)
Pin (Don Blount's ofc.)

BEN
Blue jeans
Blue striped shirt
    (Andwyneth scene and
    scene and Goodbye
    scene
Blue shirt (other scenes)
Blue jean jacket

Belt with large buckle
Cowboy boots
Cowboy hat
Sports bra
Cotton boxers
Socks?
Bolla?

JACKEY
White pleated pants
White t-shirt
White shirt
Black Shoes
Blond wig
Black Glasses
Black watch
Socks
Sports bra

RALPH
Grey plaid two piece suit
White shirt
Black belt
Black lace up shoes
Wig
Glasses
Ascot
Socks
Sports bra
Handkerchief in coat pocket?

WIKÉWITCH
Black pants
Black and white sweater

Black leather hat
Black pony tail elastic
Black loafers
Glasses

LOLA
Black skirt
Red shirt
Black Heels
Black stockings
Clip on earrings
Pin or necklace
Black bag

JOE BOB
Dockers
Short sleeve shirt
Beige hat
Sunglasses?
Saddle shoes
Socks?

JOBY
Black skirt
Multi color knit shirt
Black leather coat with
  leopard trim
Socks?
Black boots
Black glasses with gold
  trim
Black waist pack?

CASEY

#1 Audition
Black pants
Black spandex skirt
Black short sleeve
    knit top
Black shoes
White socks
Black glasses and holder
Earrings: rhinestones and
    two hoops
Red crystal bracelet
Red & Black backpack

#2 Airplane
Add black jacket

#3 Andwyneth
Remove black jacket

#4 Pajama Party
Gray and white stiped
    pj bottoms
Light green tank top
Light green hoodie
Glasses and holder
    (same)?

#5 1st Wikéwitch
    Rehearsal
Black pants (same)
White knit top
Black cropped cardigan
    sweater

White socks (same)
Black shoes (same)
Glasses and holder (same)?
    Black bag (same)
Scarf?
Bracelet (same)

#6 Work out
Grey sweat pants
Top
Hoodie
Socks (athletic)
Sneakers
Hair clips ?

#7 Goodbye and Airport
Black skirt (long)
Black and magenta top
Black boots
Magenta tights
Bracelet (same)
Glasses and holder (same)?
Black ruffley sweater
Red backpack (same)

LISABETTE

#1 Audition
Dark blue mini skirt
Light blue ruffley
    blouse
Shoes
Bracelet
Hair clips
Bag
Turquoise bra

#2 Airplane
Add Blue leather
    jacket

#3 Andwyneth
Remove Blue leather
    jacket
Remove shoes
Add cowboy boots
Add socks

#4 Pajama Party
Blue cotton boxers
White wife beater
    t-shirt
Blue bathrobe with
    ducks
Blue flip flops with
    flowers

#5 Wikéwitch
Blue jean shorts
Raspberry top with lace
Red plaid shirt
Cowboy boots
Socks
Bracelets
Hair clips

#6 Work out
Grey shorts
Actor Express t-shirt
Sneakers
Footies with balls
Ponytail

#7 Goodbye and Airport
Turquoise and white print
    skirt
White top
Cowboy boots
Socks
Turquoise bra (same)

HOLLY

#1 Audition
Thong
Black bra
Shocking Pink two
    piece suit
Black heels
Rhinestone tennis
    bracelet
Rhinestone earrings
Rhinestone necklace

#2 Airplane
Beige pleated skirt
Black v-neck top
Black leather jacket
Black heels (same)
Jewelry (same)
Bag
Black sunglasses

#3 Andwyneth
Remove Black leather
    jacket
Remove sunglasses

#4 Pajama Party
Sarong
Raspberry bra
White sht (tied in knot)
Pink glasses?

#5 Wikéwitch
Light blue "tie dye" jeans

White top
Raspberry bra
Blue sandals

#6 Fitting
Grey top with black sstraps
Grey pants
Black ankle strap shoes
Black bra (same)
Black Masha skirt
Black Masha bodice
Masha necklace?
Jewelry (same)

#6 Rehearsal
Remove Masha bodice
Remove Masha necklace?

**#7 Rehearsal with Ben and
    Love Scene**
Add gray sweater

**#8 After Love Scene, Rehearsal
    and Ben at Door**
Add beaded gray sweater

#9 Workout
Bike shorts
Bra?
Shirt
Sneakers
Footies

#10 Interview
Pink pants (from suit)
Pink top
Black heels (from 1st scene)

#11 Goodbye
Blue dress
Black bra (same)
Sandals
Jewelry (same)

#12 Airport
Add Black leather jacket
    (same)
Add Bag
Add sunglasses

Grace and Glorie
TOM ZIEGLER

"A sentimental odd-couple crowd pleaser."
THE NEW YORK TIMES

"A slick piece of entertainment."
NEW YORK DAILY NEWS

Estelle Parsons and Lucie Arnaz starred on Broadway in this charmer set in the Blue Ridge Mountains. A feisty 90-year-old cancer patient who has lived her entire life in a remote cabin and a newly transplanted urban hospice volunteer who has lost her young son confound and comfort each other as they share moments of joy and pain. The play is infused with easy humor and spicy exchanges about religion, marriage and other topics related to life's highs and lows. 2 f. (#9944)

Jack and Jill
JANE MARTIN

"An asset by virtue of its human and everyday concerns. ... A worthy play."
VARIETY

This insightful play and excellent source of scene and monologue material by the author of KEELY AND DU and VITAL SIGNS is a series of short scenes that chronicle the birth, life, death and rebirth of a relationship. Jack and Jill climb the hill of romance and marriage, but her constant need to analyze feelings sours their love. They separate for two years and then love rekindles. 1 m., 1 f., extras. (#12902)

Samuel French, Inc.
SERVING THE THEATRICAL COMMUNITY SINCE 1830

Flight
ARTHUR GIRON

"A witty, touching flashback...There is poignancy
between the laughs." —*The New York Times*

The author doesn't claim it happened exactly this way. He has
taken real-life characters and biographical information and supposed what it was like for Orville and Wilbur growing up in the
dysfunctional Wright family. They are portrayed as boys whose
mischief is just a sign of frustrated brilliance. Not a documentary,
the play explores the dynamics of the Wright family in theatrical
terms. 4 m., 1 f. (#8179)

Pride's Crossing
TINA HOWE

Best American Play of 1998
New York Drama Critics Circle
"A play you will remember and forever cherish....It is rich in both
texture and imagination."— *New York Post*
"A lovely achievement...Mabel becomes a woman who ... both
typified her time and her class and transcended it."—*Variety*

At ninety, Mabel Tidings Bigelow insists on celebrating her
daughter and granddaughter's annual visit with a croquet party. As
the party unfolds, she relives vignettes from the past that reveal the
precise moment of opportunity lost and love rejected that define
her life. The vibrant portrait of Mabel that takes shape culminates
in her one shining achievement when she became the first woman
to swim the English Channel. 4 m., 3 f. (#18230)

Samuel French, Inc.
SERVING THE THEATRICAL COMMUNITY SINCE 1830

You Shouldn't Have Told
ANNE THOMPSON-SCRETCHING

*Winner of the 1997 Jean Dalrymple Award
for Best New Playwright*
"Cyclonic.... A sometimes hilarious, often searing
portrait of black urban America in the 1990s."
—*New York Post*

Standing-room-only audiences cheered the New York production of this emotionally charged drama about a middle-class black family coping with a shameful tragedy. This is the story of a decent mother who refuses to believe her three daughters when they tell her that her boyfriend is sexually molesting them until the youngest dies from a botched abortion. It touches a nerve that crosses class and cultural experiences. 4 m., 5 f. (#27610)

Mr. Bundy
JANE MARTIN

"Jane Martin has written her strongest play yet."
—*Theatrescope*

This powerful drama examines the fears of parents driven to do "the right thing" to protect their daughter. Mom and dad learn that their neighbor is a convicted child molester and consider both vigilance and vigilantism before being forced into action by a pair of child advocacy crusaders. The shocking climax hits a nerve, leaving the audience to consider where the line between right and wrong lies. This play was a hit at the 1998 Actors Theatre of Louisville Humana Festival. 3m., 1f., 1 f. child. (#15295)

Samuel French, Inc.
SERVING THE THEATRICAL COMMUNITY SINCE 1830